NEW ZEALAND FOREST BIRDS
and their world

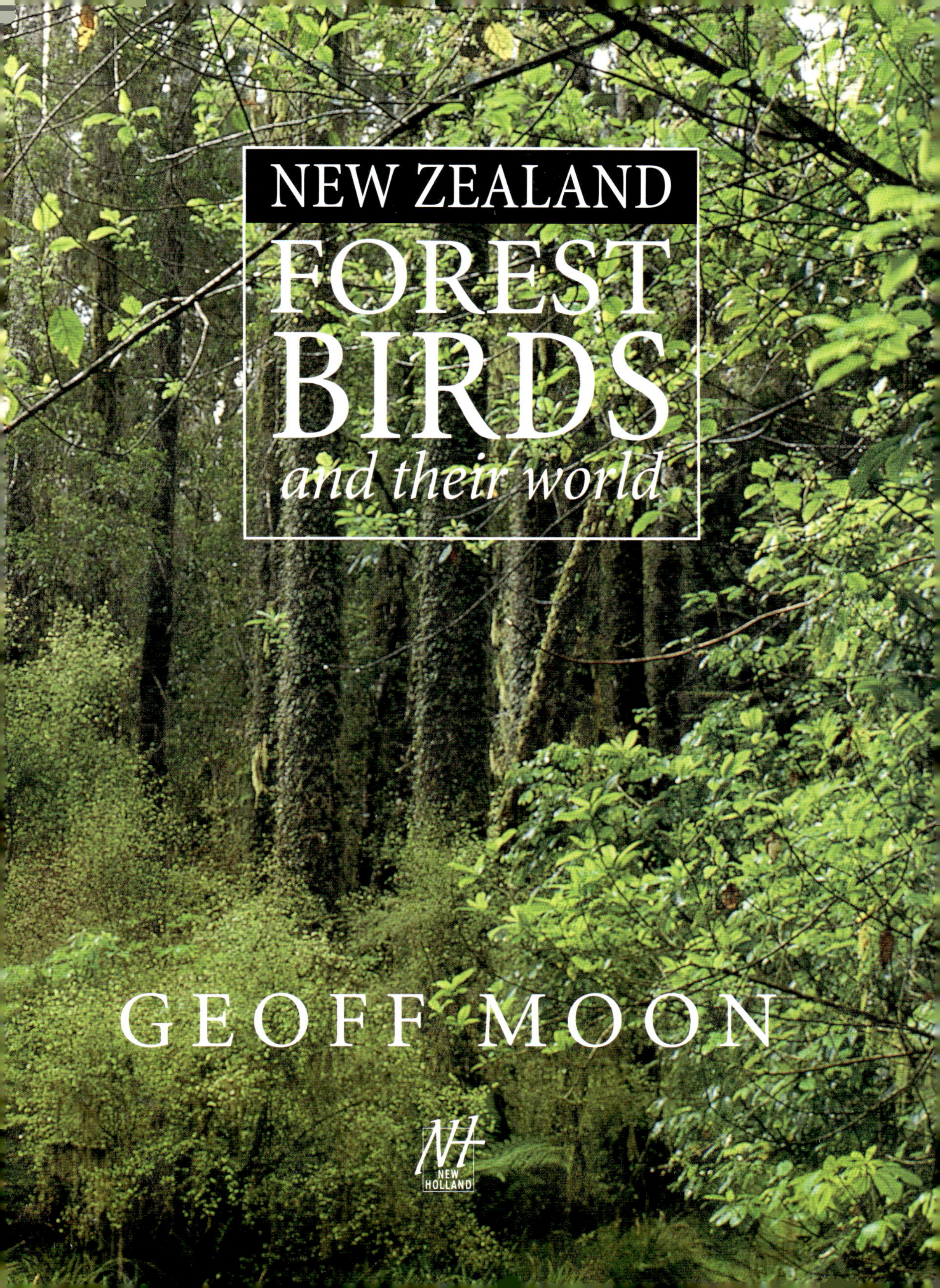

NEW ZEALAND

FOREST BIRDS

and their world

GEOFF MOON

NH NEW HOLLAND

PUBLISHERS' NOTE

Geoff Moon passed away in March 2009 during the closing stages of work on this book, his fourth to be published by New Holland. The first, *New Zealand: Land of birds*, appeared in 2001, quickly followed by *A Photographic Guide to Birds of New Zealand* (2002), and later by *New Zealand Wetland Birds and their World* (2008). Birds were Geoff's boundless passion; working with him was a pleasure and an education, and it has been deeply gratifying to be part of the process by which that pleasure and learning has passed on to his readers. The publishers offer their special thanks to Lynnette Moon, who assisted Geoff in all his work and was particularly instrumental in bringing this title to press.

ACKNOWLEDGEMENTS

There is a greater awareness now of the importance of our varied forests, as well as a concern for the wildlife that is dependent on them. Along with *New Zealand Wetland Birds and their World*, published by New Holland in 2009, Belinda Cooke and Matt Turner also encouraged me to write *Forest Birds* as a companion work. I am grateful for the opportunity they offered and for their constant support. I would like to thank the editor, Brian O'Flaherty, and others who have assisted me, as well as my wife, Lynnette, whose interest and involvement helped me to complete the book.

This is an opportunity to mention my gratitude to colleagues, photographers and others in the fields of conservation, with whom I have shared experiences over so many years. I would also like to include my appreciation for the valuable support I have received from Ray Richards and his agency over many years.

I have made many close, enduring friendships and enjoyed opportunities to join expedition teams, give lectures, visit schools and have my work made available to the public through varieties of media.

I have always considered it an honour and joy to contribute and share the knowledge and understanding I have gained with others, especially children.

Geoff Moon, February 2009

CONTENTS

Acknowledgements 5

Introduction 8

Order STRUTHIONIFORMES: **ratites (kiwi)**

Brown kiwi 26
Little spotted kiwi 30
Great spotted kiwi 32

Order FALCONIFORMES: **diurnal birds of prey**

New Zealand falcon 34

Order GRUIFORMES: **rails, swamphens and coots**

Weka 38

Order COLUMBIFORMES: **pigeons and doves**

New Zealand pigeon 43

Order PSITTACIFORMES: **cockatoos, parrots, parakeets**

North Island kaka 55
South Island kaka 60
Red-crowned parakeet 61
Yellow-crowned parakeet 68
Eastern rosella 70

Order CUCULIFORMES: **cuckoos**

Shining cuckoo 73
Long-tailed cuckoo 76

Order STRIGIFORMES: **owls**
Morepork 78
Little owl 93

Order CORACIIFORMES: **kingfishers**
New Zealand kingfisher 95

Order PASSERIFORMES: **passerine birds**
Rifleman 100
Whitehead 103
Yellowhead 105
Brown creeper 106
Grey warbler 108
Fantail 111
New Zealand tomtit 117
New Zealand robin 119
Silvereye 122
Stitchbird 124
Bellbird 126
Tui 128
Kokako 131
Saddleback 137

Glossary 140

Further Reading 140

Index 141

INTRODUCTION

New Zealand's native forests are unique and so is the avian fauna that evolved to inhabit them. Due to the geographic isolation of New Zealand, after separation from the Gondwanaland supercontinent some 80 million years ago, the forest and its birdlife evolved with an absence of browsing mammals or mammalian predators. As a consequence some of the birds are large, with a few also being flightless. Most of the birds are dull coloured, and the greatest proportion of those that inhabit native forests are endemic.

Above: Puketi Kauri Forest, Northland.

Left: Waipoua Forest, Northland, at dawn.

The New Zealand forest

Prior to the arrival of the first Polynesian settlers, New Zealand's mainland and offshore islands were densely shrouded in pristine evergreen forests. The forests were interspersed with wetlands, tussock grassland and alpine vegetation.

Kauri and mixed broadleaf forests covered much of the warmer Northland regions, including the Waitakere Ranges and Coromandel, with the mixed broadleaf forests reaching to the coasts.

Lowland forests, supporting many podocarp and hardwood trees, extended across areas such as the Waikato, Taranaki and Hawke's Bay regions, while dense wetland forests consisting mainly of kahikatea trees spread over low-lying areas, such as the Hauraki Plains or parts of the South Island west coast.

Beech forest, comprising chiefly species of *Nothofagus* beech, covered much of the higher country east of the present Tongariro National Park in the North Island, as well as extensive areas of the high country in the South Island.

Forest modification

Although some of our unlogged forests appear unmodified, none remains in a pristine state. To some degree, introduced browsing mammals have had an impact on all our forests.

According to the eminent palaeontologist and ornithologist, the late Sir Charles Fleming (writing

in Volume 1 of *Nature Heritage*), 'The arrival of Polynesian man in New Zealand, together with his dog and kiore rat, and his knowledge of fire, brought about changes in New Zealand ecology more severe than any of the violent fluctuations of climate that had taken place since the first Ice Age some 1,750,000 years ago.'

Those early settlers needed open land for habitation and gardens, but with the use of fire to clear land, these fires often burned out of control and unnecessarily destroyed much forest on the east coasts of both main islands. The forests of the Catlins, Banks Peninsula and Stewart Island escaped destruction, as did some coastal forests in the North Island.

Far left: Kauri trees in Waipoua Forest, Northland.

Left: Mixed broadleaf trees dominate the forest in the upper Waipoua River region.

Below: Almost eradicated by introduced predators, the stitchbird owes its survival to populations on predator-free islands. It is very gradually recolonising the mainland.

However, the damage caused by the early Polynesian settlers was followed by even greater devastation of the forests with the arrival of the European settlers. In addition to felling swathes of forest, these settlers also introduced many species of European passerine birds. They are thought to have transmitted avian diseases to which native birds had no resistance. Climbing ship rats had already invaded many forests, having gained access from the boats of early settlers.

Throughout the nineteenth century, settlers introduced browsing mammals such as deer, goats and pigs. Most unfortunately of all, the Australian brush-tailed possum was introduced. These mammals browsed heavily on the seeds, flowers and foliage of plants on which many native birds depended. For game purposes, the settlers also released tahr, chamois and deer to alpine regions.

Above: Hen Island. After saddlebacks became extinct on the mainland a remnant population survived on Hen Island, off the east coast of Northland.

Right: A North Island saddleback preening.

The predatory activities of rats were compounded when mustelids, such as stoats and ferrets, were introduced. Stoats, as well as taking eggs and chicks from nests, also proved adept at killing large nesting birds. From photographic evidence in recent years, even large birds such as kaka are destroyed by stoats when incubating eggs on their nests in tree hollows, from which the birds are unable to escape.

In addition to the damage to forests and their birdlife, early settlers drained wetlands extensively for agricultural use.

The forests today

It is estimated that a third of the country remains forested, most protected in national parks, reserves and conservation land. Much restoration is taking place, although many habitats are still under pressure.

Today, many of the wetland rainforests remain relatively intact, as do many of the beech and mixed forests of Fiordland. Stands of magnificent podocarp forest still survive in Te Urewera National Park, particularly the Whirinaki Forest Park. In Northland, a relentless campaign led by the late Professor W. R. McGregor resulted in the preservation of a large area of unlogged kauri, which now forms the Waipoua Forest Sanctuary.

Many stands of native forest are now protected from exploitation and some of the denuded, logged forests are regenerating. The establishment of several so-called 'mainland islands', where predators have been eliminated, and where, in

Below: North Island kaka inhabit podocarp forests.

Right: Podocarp forest in Whirinaki, Te Urewera National Park.

Overleaf: Mixed forest surrounds Lake Waikaremoana in Te Urewera National Park.

many cases, predator-proof fences have been erected, has enabled endangered bird species to be relocated in safety. The birds are transferred to these sanctuaries from offshore islands.

Research has shown that the number of resident bird species in a particular forest area is related to its size. Larger bird species, such as kaka, parakeets and kokako, do not survive in small, isolated stands of forest.

Where logging has taken place in many large tracts of forest over the years, only fragmented stands remain. These small locations of native forest support only a limited number of bird species, usually the smaller insectivorous birds, such as fantails, silvereyes and grey warblers.

Birds that are strong fliers will periodically fly to areas of seasonal flowering or fruiting trees. However, weak fliers such as kokako and saddlebacks require corridors of native trees that will allow them to move from one region of forest to another.

Indigenous birds were not genetically programmed to protect themselves against mammalian predators. In addition, human manipulation of many environments altered their chances of survival. Scientists and conservationists understand the threats to these birds and have greatly assisted in their survival, with the creation of predator-free islands, and in continued predator control within many forests.

New Zealand's primary forest types

The existing mixed podocarp and broadleaf forests of the Ureweras in the central North Island are now considered of international significance. Due to New Zealand's isolation, the remaining forests bear a resemblance to the ancient forests of the Gondwanaland supercontinent.

The mixed rainforests of Westland are penetrated by tall podocarp trees, and in the milder Paparoa Range nikau palms survive, well south of their normal range.

A combination of podocarp and broadleaf trees constitutes the forest that grows in the wetter areas east of the Southern Alps, with examples remaining in the Peel Forest today. This forest habitat is a location of native birds.

Extensive beech forests range from the central South Island to dominate the forests of Fiordland. New Zealand's beech forests comprise five different species, which are somewhat similar to

Yellow-crowned parakeet.

those found in some southern hemisphere countries, particularly South America. This link dates back to the time when New Zealand was part of Gondwanaland.

The varieties of beech grow in differing habitats, from lowland regions to more fertile, well-drained areas, as well as in wetter conditions and less fertile soils. They grow to high altitudes as far as the tree line and, like other trees at higher levels, especially in the South Island, become stunted in growth. The trees gradually merge into the alpine herbfields, the domain of the New Zealand pipit, kea and a few introduced birds such as dunnocks (hedge sparrows).

Below: The mild climate of Paparoa Range in Westland promotes the growth of nikau palms and mixed broadleaf forest, which provides a habitat for great spotted kiwi.

Exotic pine forests are now a prominent feature of the New Zealand landscape. Recent surveys have shown that the abundant insect life that exists in many of these forests attracts insectivorous native birds, especially where native shrubs and ferns also grow.

In addition, a multitude of small exotic birds, particularly seed-eating chaffinches, visit clearings in the forest, where shrubs have grown up. These birds in turn have attracted New Zealand falcons to some large pine plantations. Recent research has shown that many pairs of falcons now regularly nest on the ground in some locations where pines have been logged.

Overleaf: Beech forest covers much of Fiordland National Park.

Birds in the forest ecosystem

Petrels

In their pristine state, many of the inland forests provided suitable habitat for some species of pelagic petrels to nest. There is strong evidence that very large colonies of Cook's petrels nested far from the coast. After dark the seabirds flew in, crashing through the foliage as they located their burrow nest sites. By nesting within the forest, they inadvertently provided rich marine guano which fertilised the trees.

Today, although grey-faced petrels still nest in burrows on some coastal headlands, they suffer losses from introduced predators. Most of these pelagic birds now nest on the safety of offshore islands.

Birds of the forest

Birds are an essential part of the forest life cycle, with many trees and shrubs depending on them for the dispersal of their seeds or the pollination of their flowers. An exception is the beech forest. Flowers of beech trees are fertilised by pollen

Left: Westland rainforest.

Above: New Zealand pigeon feeding on nikau fruit.

being blown from one flower to another. The hard seeds produced by beech trees are unpalatable to birds, so these seeds are dispersed by being washed away by heavy rain, floating along small forest streams or by being blown by the wind.

Some bird species, particularly parakeets and kaka, crush seeds when eating the fruit so do not disperse whole seeds. These birds also take nectar and successfully pollinate other flowers. Kaka also scour the bark of some trees with their powerful beaks and feed on the underlying sap. Many species of fruit-eaters, notably native pigeons, swallow the fruit and seed whole and so disperse the seeds over a wide area.

The small, tasty fruits of the podocarp trees have a seed attached externally, and when the fruit is eaten, the small seed is undigested and then voided with the excreta. The seeds that are dropped by birds may be spread quite some distance from the donor tree.

Tui, bellbirds, stitchbirds, saddlebacks, silver-eyes and kokako feed on the smaller tree fruits, swallowing them whole. In addition, these birds pollinate the flowers of several trees and shrubs with the pollen that clings to their heads when they sip the flower's nectar. Only the endemic pigeon is able to swallow whole the large fruits of karaka, puriri and miro trees.

It has recently been discovered that native mistletoe flowers need to be twisted by nectar-feeding birds before the flowers will open and the birds can feed on the nectar, at the same time pollinating the flower. This action is performed only by tui and bellbirds.

As well as the true honeyeaters, being the tui, bellbird and stitchbird, several other birds, particularly kaka, regularly take nectar from a variety of flowering plants. In the beech forests, these birds also feed on honeydew, and this is especially valuable in winter when there is a scarcity of nectar.

Honeydew is produced by sap-eating scale

Left: Typical South Island beech forest.

Above: South Island tomtits are common in Westland forests.

insects. Most beech trees harbour such insects, which, after feeding on the sap and digesting it, secrete the honeydew. Rich in sugar, this provides high-energy food which is taken not only by nectar-feeding birds but also by some insect species. In recent years, particularly in the Nelson Lakes region, swarms of the introduced German wasp have seriously competed for honeydew and depleted this valuable food. The Department of Conservation is controlling the wasp menace.

The forest floor litter of dead leaves and fallen rotting branches of mature trees provides a rich habitat for varieties of invertebrates. Fungi, mosses and ferns help the old logs break down, and the insects that live there and among the decaying leaf litter in turn provide essential food for insectivorous birds that feed on the forest floor. In particular, these birds include kiwi, robins, tomtit and saddleback. Unfortunately, this has become a dangerous environment since the introduction of mammalian predators. Saddlebacks have suffered, as they spend considerable time turning over leaves on the forest floor in search of insects. In the past, this led to their extinction from mainland forests.

Introduced birds

The only introduced passerine birds that may be found in native forest are the blackbird and chaffinch. Starlings are often found within forest fringes where they make use of holes in mature trees for nesting, thus competing with some native bird species.

Chaffinches and blackbirds may be located in regions of regenerating forest, especially where this borders suburban habitat. It would seem that these species of exotic birds have found the forest a valuable source of food.

Ratites (kiwi)

The Struthioniformes contains the ratites, a group of flightless birds descended from a common ancestor that did fly, and 11 ratite species exist in the world today. They are running birds with powerful legs and reduced wings. All species lack the sternum or keel on which wing muscles are normally attached. Included in this order are the 11 species of moa which once inhabited New Zealand but are now extinct. Today, the local representatives of the order are three endemic species of kiwi, listed in Apterygidae, the oldest surviving family of New Zealand birds. (This family is sometimes put in an order of its own: Apterygiformes.)

Kiwi are quite un-birdlike and possess many unique features. For instance, they are the only birds in the world with nostrils situated at the tip of their long bills. Although they have poor eyesight, they possess acute senses of smell and hearing, similar to that of many mammals. Within thick coats of hair-like feathers are the vestiges of wings, which end in a minute claw. In addition, there are bristle-like sensory feathers around the face. Large, muscular legs and strong feet enable kiwi to run swiftly and exert forceful kicks when attacked. Female kiwi are larger than males, with a longer bill.

Kiwi inhabit a variety of forest and scrub habitats from sea level to the subalpine zone.

BROWN KIWI

Apteryx australis

Threatened; not common; widespread • Protected • Length: 40–42 cm • Maori names: kiwi (North I.), tokoeka (South I., Stewart I.), rowi (Okarito) • Status: Endemic

The brown kiwi's common name is derived from its plumage, which is brown with darker longitudinal streaks. There are three subspecies: *Apteryx australis mantelli*, in the North Island, *A. a. australis* in the South Island, and *A. a. lawryi* on Stewart Island. Of the South Island kiwi there are at least three different races. DNA tests have shown that a colony of kiwi near Okarito in Westland, where the birds are known as rowi, are probably the original kiwi. Brown kiwi that inhabit the Haast and Fiordland regions, as well as those on Stewart Island, are called tokoeka. Research and genetic studies of the different

Above: Brown kiwi are able to run fast.

Top right: An immature brown kiwi has a shorter bill.

Bottom right: Populations of brown kiwi inhabit native forests and some pine plantations in Northland, in spite of the presence of mammalian predators.

Top: Kiwi are able to locate earthworms several centimetres below the surface, by scenting them.

Above: Brown kiwi courtship.

populations continue. By recording kiwi calls from different listening points, fairly accurate counts can be made of kiwi populations in a particular locality.

Although the brown kiwi occurs on all three main islands, it has quite a restricted distribution, being most common in Northland and on Stewart Island.

Kiwi are nocturnal in habit, roosting during the day in burrows or in thick foliage. The exception is the Stewart Island brown kiwi, which often forages during the daytime, feeding on insects found along the beaches.

Male kiwi have a high-pitched call, which in the breeding season is often answered by the female's more rasping whistle. As the birds probe in the soil for prey, they snuffle noisily while exhaling to clear the nasal passages.

With their acute sense of smell kiwi can locate earthworms or insect larvae several centimetres below the surface of the ground and often thrust their long bills up to the hilt in the soft earth. In damp areas earthworms form a large part of their diet, but they also eat a wide variety of invertebrates and fallen fruit. Kiwi commonly feed in plantation pine forests on insects in the litter, with cicadas constituting a large part of the diet in these locations.

The birds nest over a prolonged season, often laying in winter months, but also in summer. Nest sites are usually located in burrows, in hollow fallen logs or among dense herbage. Brown kiwi are unusual in possessing two ovaries instead of one, enabling two eggs to be laid per clutch, although there is usually a gap of two or more weeks between the laying of the first and the second large egg. The male alone performs incubation of 75 to 85 days. On Stewart Island, however, the female, and even birds from an earlier hatch, share incubation with the male.

When hatched, the chicks have a large egg sac, which provides nourishment for several days. The chicks do not leave the nest site until five days or more old. After this they have no contact with, or feeding help from, their parents.

There is an extremely high rate of predation of

eggs and chicks by mustelids and feral cats, where present, and although adult kiwi with their powerful kick can usually protect themselves, chicks have no chance against predators. Adult kiwi are also vulnerable to attack by stray dogs, with heavy losses in some areas attributed to single roaming dogs.

To protect chicks from predation an 'Operation Nest Egg' programme is under way, with excellent results. In this scheme, eggs are removed from a burrow and incubated. The chick is then handfed and reared to an age at which it is able to fend for itself. Some chicks are temporarily relocated to predator-free islands, such as Motuora in the Hauraki Gulf. When chicks reach a weight of over 1.2 kilograms they are returned to their natal habitat, where they should be able to protect themselves from most introduced predators, although unfortunately not dogs.

A male brown kiwi broods its chick at the Otorohanga Kiwi House.

Above: A five-day-old kiwi chick leaving its burrow for the first time at night. Chicks are particularly vulnerable to predation.

LITTLE SPOTTED KIWI

Apteryx owenii

Endangered; only on predator-free islands • Protected • Length: 30 cm • Maori name: kiwi-pukupuku • Status: Endemic

The little spotted kiwi has greyish plumage with paler transverse streaks, giving it a somewhat spotted appearance. The small size of this rare species makes it especially vulnerable to predation by introduced mustelids and feral cats, and it was eliminated from most of mainland New Zealand soon after the arrival of European settlers. Fortunately, a small colony survived in forests of Westland, and, according to records, some birds were relocated to Kapiti Island where they survived and now form the main population of around a thousand birds. Had it not been for this transfer, the little spotted kiwi would now be extinct.

In recent years some of the Kapiti birds have been released on predator-free islands. These include Hen Island, Red Mercury and Tiritiri Matangi. Apart from on Hen Island, the birds are increasing in number. In summer months Hen Island lacks a good freshwater supply for kiwi. The flighted birds have access to water trapped by leaves of perching astelia and other plants.

The birds' habits have been well researched on Kapiti Island. Their diet of invertebrates appears to be similar to those of other kiwi species, and they also feed on fallen fruit of shrubs. Their call is a high-pitched, vibrating whistle, quite unlike the calls of other kiwi species.

Above left: A little spotted kiwi uses its acute senses of smell and hearing to locate insects, grubs and worms.

Above: Little spotted kiwi are found only on some offshore islands. The largest population of approximately 1000 birds inhabits Kapiti Island.

Little spotted kiwi nest in burrows from September to January, usually laying only one egg, although occasionally two-egg clutches have been recorded. The female lays the largest egg relative to body size of any bird in the world, with the egg being approximately 23 per cent of the bird's bodyweight.

The male incubates the egg for approximately 70 days. The chick leaves the nest, unaccompanied by the parents, when it is five or six days old.

GREAT SPOTTED KIWI

Apteryx haastii

Locally common • Protected
• Length: 45–47 cm • Maori name: roa
• Status: Endemic

The great spotted kiwi is the largest species of kiwi, and its greyish plumage is similar to that of the little spotted kiwi. Little is known of its habits, as it has not been adequately researched.

Reasonable numbers of great spotted kiwi survive in the forests of north-west Nelson, the Paparoa Range and the northern forests of Westland, and as far south as Arthur's Pass.

Their diet consists of earthworms and insects as well as fallen forest fruit. The birds are also reported to feed on freshwater crayfish that are taken from shallow forest streams.

The call of the male bird is a high-pitched, loud, ascending whistle. This usually produces an immediate response from the female, in a lower-pitched vibrating call. Their call somewhat resembles that of brown kiwi.

Nests are built in shallow burrows, beneath the roots of trees or sometimes in hollow fallen logs. Unlike the nesting habits of brown kiwi, only one egg is laid per clutch and the female shares incubation with the male. Incubation is reported to take around 70 to 75 days, which is shorter than that of brown kiwi.

Like all kiwi, great spotted kiwi possess strong feet that are useful in digging as well as running.

Diurnal birds of prey

Only two diurnal birds of prey inhabit New Zealand: the very common Australasian harrier and the less common endemic New Zealand falcon. Although the harrier often hawks for prey over forest canopy, it does not inhabit forests, and so is not included here.

Haast's eagle (also known as the New Zealand eagle), the world's largest bird of prey with an estimated wingspan in females of up to 2.4 metres, survived in New Zealand until its main prey, the moa, became extinct as a consequence of Maori hunting and loss of habitat.

Apart from the falcon and harrier, other birds of prey have been noted. The small Nankeen kestrel, *Falco cenchroides cenchroides*, an Australian species, is an irregular visitor that has been sighted frequently and is thought to have nested here.

NEW ZEALAND FALCON

Falco novaeseelandiae

Uncommon; widespread • Protected • Length: 43–47 cm • Maori name: karearea • Status: Endemic

Although not classed in subspecies, there are three races of the New Zealand falcon. The eastern falcon, the most common race, inhabits the high country east of the Southern Alps. This race is distinguished by having slightly more pointed wings than the other two. The southern falcon occupies forested areas of Fiordland, and the bush falcon inhabits forested regions of the North Island. However, the bush falcon is rarely seen north of the central volcanic plateau.

Falcons possess acute eyesight and fly swiftly in a direct flight, unlike the slow, gliding flight of the harrier. Also unlike the harrier, which often feeds on carrion, the falcon takes only live prey, on the wing. This is most commonly small passerine birds, although the falcon also takes larger prey such as pigeons and even pheasants. In mid-flight, falcons strike birds with their talons in a spectacular diving swoop at 200 kilometres per hour. Falcons can also fly at speed close to the ground, easily capturing prey such as rabbits. In addition to their spectacular swooping flight seen

Below, the New Zealand falcon is shown in flight while, on the right, the perched falcon displays its talons.

in the open, falcons are capable of manoeuvring easily through forest by virtue of their short wings and long tails. This great versatility in flight enables falcons to cope in many varieties of habitat.

Male falcons are smaller than females and do most of the hunting when females are tending chicks. Another example of the command of flight possessed by falcons is the manoeuvre known as 'the pass' in which the male transfers captured prey to the female in midair. Both birds fly directly towards each other and at the last second roll outwards so that their talons touch and the prey is transferred. This amazing skill is usually displayed during courtship and nesting.

Although Dr Nick Fox has extensively studied eastern falcons, until recently there has been little information on the nesting habits of the bush falcon in native forests. Nests have been located in clumps of perching astelia in forest trees, and very recently Dr Richard Seaton has made a comprehensive study of nesting bush falcons in the plantation pine forests of Kaingaroa. His research was initiated and assisted by the Wingspan Birds of Prey Trust in Ngongotaha near Rotorua, an organisation founded by the indomitable Debbie Stewart, who has reared falcon chicks from eggs found in nests on the ground in the Kaingaroa Forest.

There was one report in 1940 of a pair of falcons nesting on the ground in a plantation forest firebreak, but this was the first report of this kind. Herbert Guthrie-Smith studied bush falcons early in the twentieth century on his extensive property in Hawke's Bay. He observed several bush falcons' nests on ledges, scrappily

A captive bush falcon. The birds have a command of flight that allows them strong rapid flight above ground level to easy manoeuvrability through forests, as well as the ability to soar and dive from great heights.

covered with grasses and fern, at the base of limestone bluffs.

Falcons keep large territories and are very defensive, not tolerating intruders near nest sites. In the early 1960s my friend John Kendrick and I were observing robins as they fed on the ground in the forest of Te Urewera National Park. Near these birds was a female blackbird. Suddenly, without warning, a falcon swooped like a lightning strike and snatched the blackbird. It appeared that the falcon was nesting on the nearby Ngamoko Bluff.

Wingspan Trust has had support from timber workers in the Kaingaroa Forest, who have reported any nests located in cleared areas of the plantation forest. In 2003, 20 nests were found and studied, and this dramatically increased to 36 nests in the 2006 season. (Details of this extensive study can be obtained from Wingspan Trust, or by reading Dr Richard Seaton's PhD thesis.)

All the nests in the Kaingaroa Forest were located on the ground in logged areas. Some were found under remnants of logs or clumps of ferns among the cut-over pines, and others in more open areas.

Falcons choose these sites located on the ground where the Kaingaroa Forest has been logged for nesting because within their territory there is an abundance of small passerine birds. The most numerous of the passerine species preyed on by falcons are the introduced finches, particularly chaffinches. This habitat has proved to be a prolific feeding ground, and it is essential for successful breeding.

Where plantation forest borders native forest, bush falcons appear to prefer nesting in the native forest, often in perching astelia. Nesting behaviour at these sites has not been studied, as it would require the building of hides high in trees adjacent to the nests.

As with all falcons, no additional nesting material is used in the nest. Birds will nest on bare, high cliff ledges, as well as in trees or on the ground. The usual clutch consists of two or four eggs which are incubated mainly by the female, with the male incubating for short spells. Incubation takes 30 to 31 days. Clutches that contain four eggs probably indicate that there is a very ample supply of food prey within a reasonable distance of the nest.

Chicks are fed on fresh prey, which is first torn up and fed to them and later dangled for them to seize, helping them learn skills they will later use in maturity. The smaller male chicks fledge at 32 days of age and the larger female chicks when they are 35 days old. The chicks remain with, and are fed by, the parents for up to eight weeks.

Rails, swamphens and coots

The only New Zealand forest bird included in this order is the endemic rail, the weka, of the genus *Gallirallus*.

Most of the species in this order have a strong homing instinct, and although not web-footed, many are good swimmers. The weka has reasonably developed wings but it is flightless.

WEKA

Gallirallus australis

Endangered; widespread • Protected • Length: 53 cm • Status: Endemic

Weka, also known as woodhens, are not strictly forest birds. But they are included in this book because, similar to kingfishers, weka inhabit a range of locations. These include the coast, open country, forest and many offshore islands. They are large, flightless birds with strong legs, a stout bill, and short, rounded wings.

There are four subspecies of the endemic weka, which vary slightly in size and colouration: buff weka (*Gallirallus australis hectori*), western weka (*G. a. australis*), North Island weka (*G. a. greyi*) and Stewart Island weka (*G. a. scotti*).

Although the buff weka became extinct in the South Island, it is now very common in the Chatham Islands where it was introduced. Western weka inhabit the north-west of the South Island, Westland and Fiordland. In Fiordland they are dimorphic in plumage, with some birds having very dark plumage. North Island weka, introduced to Kawau Island and parts of Northland, were once very common in the Poverty Bay region. But, as has occurred in some other regions, the populations rapidly declined, possibly due to drought conditions, predation or disease. The Stewart Island subspecies is now present only on islands off Stewart Island, and for protection it was introduced to Kapiti Island.

Left: Weka nest under tree roots, logs and in thick clumps of vegetation.

Below: A North Island weka foraging for insects and seeds among vegetation.

In the late 1950s weka were very common in the Gisborne district and frequently caused damage to suburban gardens. The Wildlife Department, as it was known at the time, trapped several birds and wished to relocate them. I was asked to release some birds in the Rodney district north of Auckland. Soon, 40 birds that had been fitted with leg identification bands arrived by airfreight.

As I was extremely busy at that time of year in my veterinary practice, I was unable to make a 'soft' release by keeping them in an aviary for a week or more. So I released them all in what I considered was an ideal habitat in the Dome Valley, about 7 kilometres north of Warkworth. In this release area there were good locations of native forest, a small river, manuka scrub and open pasture.

However, the weka's strong homing instinct was soon demonstrated when, early the next morning, I received a call from a neighbour in Warkworth to tell me that a banded weka had appeared in his garden. The bird was apparently progressing south, and had swum the tidal Mahurangi River.

I was even more surprised to receive a call the following day from a farmer at Puhoi who reported that two weka were in one of his paddocks. These birds were also apparently heading home to Gisborne!

The only survivors from this attempted translocation were, reportedly, a pair breeding at Leigh, and another pair with chicks near Waipu in the north. Mammalian predators possibly killed the birds that had returned south. Some years later I photographed a nesting pair in the Bay of Islands region. These birds were probably the result of a later translocation.

At the time of writing, weka are reasonably common on Kawau Island. However, the birds are not welcome on smaller islands, due to their

Weka chicks are active soon after hatching, remaining with parents for several weeks. Parents allow young chicks to hitch a ride among their feathers.

habits of predation, either of eggs or chicks of ground-nesting birds and nesting petrels. Weka are also omnivorous feeders, taking fruit, seeds, insects and other invertebrates. In addition, the birds are known to eat lizards, and sometimes catch mice and even rats.

Weka have a very extended nesting season, with most nests being found from September to January. They lay up to five eggs in nests that are composed of grasses and dead herbage. These nests are hidden under logs or the exposed roots of large trees, or hidden in thick herbage.

Both birds share incubation for about 26 days. The chicks, clothed in sooty-coloured down, are active soon after hatching and spend several weeks foraging with their parents.

Top: Chicks are precocial and feed with a parent.

Above: A weka with its older chick.

Pigeons and doves

Only one common native pigeon, the kereru or kukupa, inhabits New Zealand. A slightly larger but rare subspecies, the Chatham Island pigeon or parea, *Hemiphaga chathamensis*, survives in small but slowly increasing numbers and is confined to the Chatham Islands.

Apart from our true forest pigeon, the introduced rock dove or feral pigeon is very common and widespread, particularly in suburban parks. But this pigeon is a grain feeder and does not enter forests.

Two introduced doves, the Malaysian spotted dove, *Streptopelia chinensis tigrina*, and the barbary dove, *S. roseogrisea*, are increasing in numbers. The former is the most common and sometimes nests in shrubs or among vines in forest margins, but neither of these species eats fruit and so they do not compete with our endemic pigeon.

NEW ZEALAND PIGEON

Hemiphaga novaeseelandiae novaeseelandiae

Common; widespread (except in beech forest and alpine habitats) • Protected • Length: 52 cm • Maori name: kereru, kukupa • Status: Endemic

A New Zealand pigeon.

New Zealand pigeons favour mixed forests, primarily broadleaf and podocarp forests, as these trees produce a greater abundance of fruit. The birds are also sometimes seen in more open country, as long as they have access to nearby 'food trees'. They are not found in pure beech forest, because of a lack of suitable fruiting trees.

New Zealand pigeons are widely distributed in forests throughout the country, as well as in forest remnants. Originally, they were particularly plentiful in the north of the North Island, where the forest suited their needs, especially the great 'food tree', the puriri, but due to continued hunting of this plump, easy target, the birds have diminished in number in the far north.

These birds are of prime ecological importance, as they feed on a wide variety of shrub and tree fruit, without crushing the seeds. The undamaged seeds are then defecated by the pigeon and dispersed over wide areas, helping to maintain regeneration of our native forests. They are the only birds that are able to swallow whole the largest native tree fruits such as karaka and puriri.

The birds also eat sprouting leaves and flowers of kowhai and take advantage of many fruit of introduced exotic plants, unfortunately spreading the seeds of the exotic *Acmena* (lilly pilly or monkey apple) fruits in some areas of regenerating forest. White clover flowers of pastures often attract pigeons to feed on the ground, particularly on safe, predator-free islands.

When drinking, pigeons keep their heads lowered as they suck up water, not dipping and raising their heads, as do other birds.

New Zealand pigeons are strong fliers, and although they usually feed close to their nesting locations, large flocks can often be seen flying to other areas of fruiting trees.

I have often watched pigeons feeding on kahikatea fruit from a large tree in our garden. I have recorded that they feed for up to four minutes to fill their crop, then sit relaxed, digesting the food for several minutes before beginning another feeding session. As the large birds feed on fruit in leafy trees such as pigeonwood, or in the canopy of other trees, they often remain unseen. But they soon reveal their presence when their heavy rustling movements through the foliage result in swaying branches and ripe fruits dropping to the ground.

In flight, native pigeons are readily noticeable, with the low, whistling sounds produced by their heavy wing-beats. Their rounded wings enable them to fly among foliage trees, with minimum ripple to the leaves.

The birds' spectacular aerial display flights are often thought to be a courtship spectacle, yet, overlooking a large area of native forest from my house, I have watched the display during several months of the year. The aerial manoeuvre begins with fast wing flapping to rise for a downward glide, and then curving upwards to gain height and almost stalling before making a downward plunge into the forest canopy.

New Zealand pigeons have an extended nesting season, which varies according to the availability of suitable food. I have seen nests in early September and as late as February. Nests are usually flimsy structures composed of sticks and built in the upper branches of tall shrubs, in the crowns

Left: New Zealand pigeons are heavy and clamber on tree foliage as they search for food. This makes them vulnerable to predators.

Following pages: New Zealand pigeon feeding on an abundant crop of nikau berries.

Above: New Zealand pigeon feeding on pigeonwood fruit.

Right: The male pigeon brings a stick at changeover time during incubation of the single egg.

of nikau palms or in the forks of large trees. Macrocarpas are a prime site in northern regions, as are *Acmena* and bushy totara trees. Only one white egg is laid per clutch, which is incubated by both parents in turn for up to 30 days.

Three nests that I had under observation were all fairly close to a road I frequently used, so I was able to check developments during the day. The male appeared to incubate from about 9 am to 4 or 5 pm. Although not banded for identification, one pair was particularly suitable for observation as each bird showed a marked behavioural difference. The female, in true pigeon fashion, did not leave the nest when I inspected the egg, just striking my hand with her wing. But the second bird, which I assumed was the male, always left the nest when I started to climb the tree, but returned to incubate as soon I climbed down. In another nest, the female had a light mark at the side of her head, which identified her.

Although most nests are flimsy structures, some are reasonably substantial and probably built by older birds. On one occasion, I was observing nesting parakeets from a hide. A pigeon was nesting in an adjacent pohutukawa tree, giving me a clear view of the nest. I was able to watch the changeover of a morning shift, when what I considered to be the male bird came onto the nest. I expected the female, who had been incubating all night, to fly off to feed. Instead, she flew to a large kanuka tree and broke off a dead twig about 15 centimetres in length and brought it to the nest. She repeated the procedure five times before flying off. The male bird continued to sit with the pile of sticks close to him, yet it was fully 15 minutes before he made a rough

attempt to arrange the sticks around the side of the nest.

Little was known of the New Zealand pigeon's feeding of the chick. Guthrie-Smith spent several hours in hides without witnessing feeding, and thought the chick must be fed at night. However, he eventually succeeded in watching a chick being fed, and obtained a photograph during the day.

Soon after hatching, a pigeon chick is fed by the regurgitation of a milky secretion from the parent's crop. This protein-rich secretion is somewhat similar in composition to mammalian milk. As the chick grows, the milk is supplemented

Left top and bottom: Prior to feeding, the parent grips the chick's bill crosswise before regurgitating food.

Below: Some of the pigeon milk and fruit pulp is spilt when feeding the chick. It resembles porridge in consistency. The birds fly long distances to source fruits, buds and foliage which they gather from trees, not from the ground.

by the addition of various partly digested fruits, and after it is about four weeks of age the chick is fed on regurgitated whole fruits. During warmer months, when about five or six days old, the chick is fed soon after dawn, and then left unattended for most of the day.

With my early observations of nesting birds, I spent several hours at a time in hides. From early morning I watched a six-day-old chick alone in the nest, and when the parent finally arrived at the nest in the evening, the chick, which had not been fed since early morning, made no demand to be fed, but just snuggled under the parent. However, it has yet to be determined if the chick is fed during the night.

To record the feeding of chicks in different nests, on several occasions I entered the bush just before dawn and sat down about 20 metres from the hide to await the sitting bird's departure to feed. In summer the bird usually left soon after 4.30 am when dawn was breaking and flew into the bush canopy to feed. I then entered the hide and quickly set up camera and flash, using a torch shone on the nest to focus my camera. From my experience, it seemed that when the chicks were about four or five days old, the parent often waited a few minutes before returning to feed. This period is probably necessary to partly digest the fruits before feeding the chick. However, when the chick is about six days old this period is considerably shortened.

When pigeons nest early in the season, it is likely that they may then nest a second time, while the first chick is still in the original nest. I have strong evidence of this, as one female I observed had an identifiable light marking on her head. When her first chick was only a few days old, I noticed her incubating on another nest nearby.

The presence of a flying pigeon is usually apparent by its loud, whistling wing-beats. Yet its approach to the nest is completely silent. The first indication I had that the parent was approaching the nest was the chick's behaviour. It started to squeak and vibrate its wings and faced the branch where the parent was expected to land. After uttering a soft 'kuu-kuu', the parent sidestepped

A New Zealand pigeon feeding a chick, five and a half weeks old.

along the branch onto the nest. Without pausing, she tapped the chick's bill, seized it crosswise and began to forcefully regurgitate with between 11 and 18 rhythmic movements. Then, after a pause of about six to eight seconds, the process was repeated. The age of the chick determined the number of times this process was repeated, which ranged from four to nine.

Although the chick's crop was visibly distended after feeding, I was surprised to find, on two occasions, that the other parent arrived to feed the chick similarly soon afterwards. At close quarters I was able to positively identify it as a different bird in each case.

On one occasion when the chick's beak was not engaged with its parent's, some of the regurgitated food spilt onto the side of the nest. When the parent had left the nest I inspected some of this material. It was the consistency of porridge and had a faint fruity smell.

As a veterinarian, I have often had injured or orphaned birds brought to my attention. In several instances it was a pigeon chick that had fallen from a nest. I found these birds very easy to care for, and although some younger ones became obviously imprinted, they were free to fly around my garden and area of bush. When fully grown the birds sometimes returned unexpectedly, and seemed eager to receive a feed of raisins or banana, their favourite foods. I have a photograph of one bird perched on my knee while I was seated on the terrace writing, and another bird chose to roost in my garage if the door was left open.

As mentioned earlier, the beautiful New Zealand pigeon is a highly important link in our ecosystem and is responsible for helping to regenerate our native forests. However, while the species is fully protected by law, in some regions, particularly Northland, many birds are hunted illegally. They also have to contend with introduced mammalian predators, especially feral cats and stoats, and competition from possums for some essential foods.

Cockatoos, parrots, parakeets

Several species and subspecies of parakeet inhabit the Chatham Islands and some subantarctic islands. However, this section will discuss only the forest inhabitants of the North, South and Stewart Islands.

It is important to mention the rare nocturnal, flightless kakapo, *Strigops habroptilus*, which is also the heaviest parrot in the world, and was once a common forest bird in the South Island.

At the turn of the twentieth century, Richard Henry, the first South Island government-appointed ranger, noticed that a stoat invasion was causing a rapid decline in the population of the kakapo, which at this time was a common bush bird. He caught more than 400 kakapo, relocating them to what he considered was the safe habitat of Resolution Island in Dusky Sound. However, stoats eventually swam to the island and eliminated the kakapo.

In 1975, I joined search parties of the Wildlife Department in an effort to trace the kakapo's last retreats in Fiordland. Unfortunately, only a few male kakapo were found and it appeared that extinction was imminent.

However, a small population of kakapo, including females, was discovered in a remote area of Stewart Island where the birds were nesting. But because their numbers were rapidly falling due to predation by feral cats, the birds were caught and transferred to predator-free islands. Today, kakapo are being intensively managed on three predator-free islands off Stewart Island and Fiordland, with the result that their numbers are now gradually increasing (124 in August 2009).

On mainland New Zealand and offshore-forested islands, kaka, *Nestor meridionalis*, are found in reasonable numbers. The kea, *N. notabilis*, is a close relative of the kaka. Although often seen in beech-forest margins, it is not a forest bird but, rather, an alpine parrot and inhabits the South Island high country.

The red-crowned parakeet, *Cyanoramphus novaezelandiae*, is also numerous on offshore islands but, due to its habit of feeding on the ground, is subject to predation by mustelids and feral cats. This parakeet is rare on the mainland.

The slightly smaller yellow-crowned parakeet, *C. auriceps*, which has different feeding habits, still survives in reasonable numbers and can often be seen or heard feeding in the canopy of forests. However, the species is not as numerous as the red-crowned parakeet on offshore islands.

The introduced eastern rosella, *Platycercus eximius*, is common and appears to be increasing in numbers in some forested regions. It competes for food and nesting sites with some native birds.

There are a few colonies of sulphur-crested cockatoo, *Cacatua galerita*, in New Zealand, which probably originated from escaped cage birds. The largest colony inhabits the west coast of the North Island south of Waikato Heads. Small numbers have been observed south of Muriwai and some in the Wairarapa. They feed mainly in open country and nest in the hollows of mature trees on forest fringes.

NORTH ISLAND KAKA

Nestor meridionalis septentrionalis

Locally common; widespread • Protected • Length: 45 cm • Status: Endemic

North Island kaka inhabit large tracts of native forest on the North Island mainland and are common on many forested offshore islands, particularly in the Hauraki Gulf, such as Great Barrier, Little Barrier and Hen Islands. Being strong fliers, some birds migrate from these islands to feed on exotic plants in Auckland suburban gardens, particularly during winter months. These will quite often be young birds, having been encouraged to seek other territory.

Often flying at night, kaka utter harsh, grating contact calls. However, particularly during the nesting season, the birds call in soft musical whistles and warbles. Kaka make quite direct flights, revealing the rich crimson and gold

A North Island kaka. These birds prefer to feed in the upper canopy.

Left: The kaka's strong bill is ideal for eating foliage and fruit and is used to extract huhu grubs from rotting wood.

Above: Abrasions (scours) in the bark of a pohutukawa tree are a sign of kaka feeding on sap.

colouring of their rounded underwings.

Kaka are mainly vegetarian feeders, taking succulent buds and foliage, various kinds of fruit and nectar. They also use their strong hooked bills to tear the bark from rotting trees to extract huhu grubs and other insect larvae.

On Hen Island I was puzzled to note deep parallel scratches in the bark of a pohutukawa trunk. I understood the reason for the marks when some days later I watched a kaka scratching the bark of a tree, and then, with its brush tongue, feeding on the sap.

Kaka begin nesting in early summer, choosing a cavity in a tree. In northern districts the holes in old puriri or pohutukawa trees are favourite sites. Often the entrance hole used is surprisingly

narrow. In one instance the widest part of an entrance hole in a puriri tree was no more than 5 centimetres across, the length of a matchbox. I noticed that, when exiting the nest, this kaka gripped the bark of the tree and seemed to squeeze out of the hole. Kaka, like other parrots, are long-lived birds. The pair I was observing had probably used this nesting cavity over several seasons, and as the tree bark gradually grew over the hole the entrance became restricted.

The three or four white eggs are laid on a bed of wood dust with no added nesting material. Only the female performs incubation, and the eggs take about 26 days to hatch. The male feeds the

Left: A female kaka about to enter her nest hole in a puriri tree.

Above: Leaving a nest entrance only 5 cm in width, she grips the bark for assistance.

incubating bird every one to one and a half hours. From a nearby branch he calls with a musical 'oowit'. The female joins him and crouches on the branch, wings quivering, tail fanned and uttering chick-like squeaks to receive regurgitated food. The process lasts about four minutes. Depending on the stage of incubation, nesting birds would immediately return to the nest, or at other times the female would fly off with her mate, being away for about 10 minutes before returning.

Soon after the chicks have hatched, the female receives the regurgitated food from the male and then immediately returns to the nest to feed the squeaking chicks. When chicks are older the female often may be away feeding, and sometimes the male might arrive to call her from the nest. However, if there is no response he will enter the nest and feed the chicks, as their squeaks can be heard easily.

Chicks leave the nest when about 10 weeks old. At this stage they cannot fly, so they perch on low shrubs or even on the ground, where the parents feed them. At this time they are very vulnerable to attack by mammalian predators.

With losses of kaka on the mainland to predation, it is the survival of good populations on our forested offshore islands that will eventually populate the growing number of 'mainland island' refuges and predator-free habitats, such as Ark in the Park in the Waitakere Ranges.

SOUTH ISLAND KAKA

Nestor meridionalis meridionalis

Widespread in South I. • Protected
• Length: 46 cm • Status: Endemic

South Island kaka, which are slightly larger than their North Island cousins, are confined to the forests of Westland, Fiordland and northern forests of the South Island. They are absent from the eastern side of the Southern Alps, but they are common on Stewart Island. Generally their numbers are thought to be decreasing.

The feeding habits of the South Island kaka are similar to those of the North Island species. In addition they feed on the nectar of flowering rata and honeydew from the bark of beech trees. In recent years, however, there is competition for the honeydew from exotic wasps, which are being controlled by poisoning. Kaka also eat insects and particularly their larvae, gouging them from rotting trees with their powerful hooked bills.

South Island kaka begin nesting in October, choosing dry cavities in mature trees. Up to five eggs are laid on a bed of powdered wood and incubated by the female for up to 25 days. As incubation commences before the clutch is complete, the last chicks to hatch, being less developed, often do not survive.

While incubating, the female is called from the nest to be fed on regurgitated food by the male. Chicks are fed on regurgitated vegetable and fruit material as well as insects and grubs. They fledge when about four to five weeks old and remain with the parents for several months.

As the nests are in confined spaces of hollow trees, the sitting bird has no way to escape from a stoat attack. Several cases recorded with cameras have shown adult female kaka and chicks killed on their nests by stoats.

The male kaka calls the female from the nest to feed her.

RED-CROWNED PARAKEET

Cyanoramphus novaezelandiae novaezelandiae

Common on many offshore islands • Protected • Length: male 25 cm; female 28 cm • Maori name: kakariki • Status: Endemic

Although the red-crowned parakeet is very common on many offshore islands and reasonable numbers inhabit the forests of Stewart Island, it is very rarely seen on the mainland. This may be due to its habit of feeding on the ground, where feral cats and stoats can easily attack it. The only time I have seen birds on the mainland was in 1980, when I observed three birds together in the Mangamuka bush in Northland.

Small numbers of these parakeets still inhabit forests in north-west Nelson, and planned releases in the larger 'mainland island' refuges are expected to be successful.

Below: A red-crowned parakeet outside its nest hole in a pohutukawa tree.

Following pages: Red-crowned parakeets thrive only where there is protection from predators, because of their tendency to feed on the ground.

Above: Red-crowned parakeets will fly long distances to reach good sources of food or fresh water.

Right: A red-crowned parakeet at its nest with chicks, which will fledge when six or seven weeks old.

The diet of the red-crowned parakeet differs from that of its close relative, the yellow-crowned parakeet. These birds feed on buds and tender shoots of foliage, and the fruit of trees and shrubs, as well as a few flowers and nectar. They are particularly fond of the seeds of flax, and when large numbers of them are feeding on the seeds, they prevent the access of honeyeaters to the flax flower nectar. During the nesting season, red-crowned parakeet also feed on insects and other invertebrates. Many years ago, when they were common on the mainland, they caused considerable damage in orchards.

Red-crowned parakeet nest from October to January, and when food is plentiful, some early nesters rear a second clutch. They prefer the

Right: Male and female red-crowned parakeets at their nest.

Below: The male has just called the female from the nest to feed her.

Far right: He feeds her by regurgitation.

hollows of mature trees or cavities of broken tree limbs and lay large clutches of up to nine eggs on bare wood pulp. On some offshore islands where there are no mature trees, the birds sometimes nest on the ground, in burrows, or in rock fissures. Incubation, by the female alone, takes just over three weeks. The chicks fledge when they are about six or seven weeks old, but it is rare for more than two or three chicks to survive. One reason for this is a shortage of food.

When the female is incubating, the male calls her from the nest every hour or so and feeds her by regurgitation. This process lasts about four minutes, with the female crouching, quivering her wings and squeaking.

After the chicks have hatched, if the female is off the nest feeding, the male calls several times with a repeated, subdued 'ki-ki-ki' call, and if the female does not appear, he enters the nest and feeds the chicks.

After fledging, the chicks feed with the parents for several weeks.

YELLOW-CROWNED PARAKEET

Cyanoramphus auriceps auriceps

Uncommon; widespread • Protected
• Length: 24–27 cm • Maori name: kakariki
• Status: Endemic

Yellow-crowned parakeets inhabit the forests of north-west Nelson, southern Westland, Fiordland and Stewart Island. In the North Island they are found in the beech forests of the Raukumara Range, Kaimanawa Mountains and Urewera ranges. The birds are far less common than red-crowned parakeets on offshore islands, where there have been reports of occasional interbreeding of the two species.

Yellow-crowned parakeets differ in feeding habits from the red-crowned parakeets, often feeding in the canopy trees of forests, where they take invertebrates. The birds particularly favour green scale insects found on the undersides of foliage leaves. They also feed on seeds, fruit and buds of shrubs.

As they feed in the canopy, yellow-crowned parakeets are more likely to be heard calling with subdued chattering before they are seen.

As with other parakeets, they choose to nest in cavities of mature trees, laying clutches of up to eight eggs, which are incubated by the female for 22 days. The male calls the female from the nest at approximately hourly intervals and feeds her with regurgitated food. When the chicks are newly hatched, the female returns to the nest immediately after the male has fed her. But when the chicks are older, the female feeds by herself and may be away longer, so the male often enters the nest to feed the chicks. Usually only two or three chicks survive to fledge when they are about 45 days old. They stay with their parents for several weeks.

The yellow-crowned parakeet is not as readily seen as the red-crowned, particularly as they frequent beech forest and feed in the upper canopy of forests.

The smaller orange-fronted parakeet, *Cyanoramphus malherbi*, was once considered to be a colour morph of the yellow-crowned parakeet, but recent DNA tests have shown it to be a distinct species. Small numbers of the birds inhabit a forested area in North Canterbury, where intensive predator control is being carried out. Their numbers in this area are increasing.

EASTERN ROSELLA

Platycercus eximius

Mainly in North I., and Otago
• Not protected • Length: 32 cm
• Status: Introduced

The expanding population of rosella parakeets, an Australian species, probably originated from escaped cage birds. Today they are common in open country where there are sheltering trees, and also in forests, particularly those of Northland and the Waitakere Ranges. They are also becoming common in some locations in the Wairarapa where there are ample stands of trees. Eastern rosella are uncommon in the South Island except for south-east Otago.

The birds feed on vegetation, fruit and seeds, and in open country often take the seeds of Scotch thistles. I have rarely seen them feeding on the ripe fruit of podocarp trees, but the birds will regularly forage on the ground for fallen seeds of kahikatea fruit in early winter months. They also cause damage in some citrus orchards in Northland by selectively feeding on new shoots and buds, as well as fruit.

Rosella parakeets obviously compete for food with our native birds and, like starlings, are particularly competitive when nesting in cavities and holes of native trees.

An eastern rosella parakeet about to enter its nest in a dead tree-fern trunk.

Their calls vary in different localities. Usually the birds call with a three-syllable whistle, and at other times in excited chatterings, as well as with screeches when alarmed.

In the north I have located most nests in the broken-off trunks of tree ferns; it is surprising that these sites should be chosen, as the birds' long tails get damaged with frequent entries and exits.

Up to six eggs are laid on the bare wood pulp from October to January, and the female incubates the clutch for 23 days. The female is called from the nest at intervals of over an hour and fed on regurgitated food by the male. Chicks fledge when they are about four weeks of age and continue to feed with their parents for several weeks before dispersing.

Rosella parakeets compete for food and nest holes with some other native birds.

Order Cuculiformes

Cuckoos

Only two members of this order are regular visitors to New Zealand each spring. However, on occasion, stragglers of some Australian cuckoo species have been recorded in New Zealand.

Cuckoos are parasitic and do not build nests or incubate their eggs. Instead, they lay one egg in each of several nests of certain species of New Zealand endemic birds. They then leave the foster parent to incubate their eggs and rear the chicks. The cuckoo chick is always much larger than its foster parent.

The small shining cuckoo, *Chrysococcyx lucidus*, which migrates here each September, chooses the nests of grey warblers in which to lay its eggs. The large long-tailed cuckoo, *Eudynamys taitensis*, which arrives in November, lays its eggs in nests of whiteheads in the North Island. In the South Island these cuckoos choose to lay their eggs in nests of brown creepers or the endangered yellowhead.

In late summer, both species return to the Solomon, Indonesia, the Bismarck Archipelago and a number of other tropical Pacific islands. Some young cuckoos have been reported to overwinter in New Zealand. In some of the islands, extensive logging of the forests is increasing. The loss of forest habitat may have a deleterious effect on the population of these cuckoo species.

SHINING CUCKOO

Chrysococcyx lucidus lucidus

Common; widespread • Protected
• Length: 16 cm • Maori name: pipiwharauroa
• Status: Native

This small cuckoo arrives each September from the tropical Solomon Islands, islands of the Bismarck Archipelago, and some other Pacific islands. It announces its presence in New Zealand with a repeated whistle of rising notes and then a descending inflection of two or three notes. The pitch is very similar to the song of the introduced song thrush when heard from a distance.

Shining cuckoos are common in all parts of New Zealand that are inhabited by grey warblers, which are the foster parents for their chicks. Early one November, a friend and I were watching brown creepers in the area known as Kowhai

A shining cuckoo. 'Shining' refers to the metallic-green sheen of the bird's wings.

The sparrow-sized shining cuckoo flies rapidly and is well camouflaged in the foliage.

Bush near Kaikoura. One of these birds was near us when suddenly a shining cuckoo landed on a branch only 4 metres away, allowing us to take a few photos before it flew off. I am not aware that these cuckoos parasitise brown creeper nests.

Shining cuckoos feed on a variety of insects, and they are one of the few birds to feed regularly on hairy caterpillars.

Grey warblers nest about three times a year, the first in August. The early nests escape attention from the cuckoo, but the second nesting in late October or November is the one that interests the cuckoo. A single egg is laid in the nests of more than one warbler nest. At the time of writing, it has not been determined how the egg is inserted into the domed nest of the warbler.

The dark greenish-coloured egg is slightly larger than that of the warbler, which then incubates it for about 15 days. This is also a shorter incubation period than that of the warbler. After the cuckoo hatches, and when just a few days old, the large chick ejects the remaining warbler eggs by lifting them, one at a time, on its back.

The cuckoo is fed at frequent intervals by the small foster parents, and finally fledges when it is nearly three weeks old. The chick calls incessantly for food and is fed by the warblers on insect food until it learns to feed itself.

On one occasion, a neighbour phoned me to watch two identical-sized shining cuckoo chicks being fed by a pair of grey warblers. I believe in this instance a cuckoo chick from another nest joined the first chick. I am sure its foster parents were relieved to transfer ownership of their foster chick.

Shining cuckoos cease calling in summer and leave New Zealand to return to their tropical winter haunts. A few birds overwinter in New Zealand, but they are silent and inconspicuous at this time.

LONG-TAILED CUCKOO

Eudynamys taitensis

Common • Protected
• Length: 40 cm • Maori name: koekoea
• Status: Endemic

The long-tailed cuckoo is much larger than the shining cuckoo. Its brown plumage with lighter brown streaks, and very long brown tail with dark bars, gives the bird a hawk-like appearance. The tail is slightly longer than the body.

After wintering in the Bismarck Archipelago and other tropical Pacific islands, most long-tailed cuckoos arrive in the North Island in October and settle in habitats occupied by whiteheads, the future foster parents chosen to incubate their eggs and rear their chicks. Others move to the South and Stewart Islands to parasitise brown creepers and yellowheads.

Long-tailed cuckoos feed on insects and spiders. Their strong hooked beaks are also used to capture larger prey such as lizards and occasionally small birds and their eggs.

The birds' usual repeated call is a steamy whistle. They also make metallic-sounding calls and shrieks, especially in late summer when they tend to form small flocks before leaving New Zealand in autumn.

Long-tailed cuckoos' calls are frequently heard, yet the birds, although conspicuous in flight, are notoriously difficult to see when perched in trees. Once, a bird was repeatedly calling from a pohutukawa tree outside the bunkhouse on Little Barrier Island. A large group of birdwatchers surrounded the tree, yet the calling bird was not seen until it flew off.

There is little information on the method used by this cuckoo to deposit its egg in various nests of whitehead, yellowhead or brown creeper. The birds lay their eggs in November leaving one in each of several nests. The cream-coloured egg with brown markings is larger than those of the parasitised recipient, which incubates it for 16 days. Eventually, the very large chick leaves the nest when about three weeks old and continues to be fed by its foster parents until it learns to find food for itself.

Long-tailed cuckoos generally return to their tropical wintering forests in early autumn, yet some birds have been observed overwintering in New Zealand.

Below: The long tail of the cuckoo is conspicuous in flight.

Right: The long-tailed cuckoo has a strong hooked beak and is able to capture prey such as lizards and small birds, as well as insects and spiders.

Owls

The morepork, *Ninox novaeseelandiae*, is the only native owl in New Zealand. The larger endemic laughing owl, *Sceloglaux albifacies*, is considered to be extinct, the last specimen being found in the South Island in 1914.

The little or German owl, *Athene noctua*, was introduced to the South Island in 1906 and is now common in eastern areas of the South Island. Apart from captive birds, the little owl does not inhabit the North Island.

The Australian barn owl, *Tyto alba delicatula*, which is a subspecies of the worldwide species *Tyto alba*, was first recorded in Australia in the early twentieth century and has occasionally been recorded in New Zealand. In the late summer of 2008, three barn owls were sighted near Kaitaia in Northland. One had a broken wing and was rescued and treated, and at the time of writing is resident at the Wingspan Birds of Prey Trust's raptor centre in Ngongotaha.

Owls are found on all continents of the world except Antarctica. Superficially they share some physical features with birds of the Falconiformes order, such as the hawks. Like them, owls possess powerful, sharp talons and strong hooked beaks designed for capturing and killing live prey.

However, in contrast to other birds of prey, owls have other unusual physical features. Most, but not all, owls are nocturnal, with only a few species hunting during daylight hours. Owls' large eyes are immovable in their skulls, so to compensate for this, the birds are able to revolve their heads 270 degrees. They achieve this because, unlike mammals, which have seven cervical vertebrae or neck bones, owls have 14. By revolving their heads, the birds are able to follow their prey or detect intruders in their territories.

Their external ear openings are large and disproportionate in size, which allows them to accurately pinpoint prey and even, for example, the position of a moving insect.

Also, due to the downy edges and surfaces of their large rounded wings, owls' wing-beats are completely silent. All these physical features make owls extremely efficient predators, enabling them, together with other predators, to maintain a balance in nature. Unfortunately, this balance has, in many countries, been upset by the introduction of exotic animals. In New Zealand, species of exotic flora and fauna have severely upset the equilibrium, resulting in the extinction of many species, and the need to protect others by expensive pest-control measures.

MOREPORK
Ninox novaeseelandiae

Common; widespread • Protected • Length: 29 cm • Maori name: ruru • Status: Native

The morepork, New Zealand's only native owl, is relatively common in forests and sheltered open country throughout the North and South Islands, offshore islands and Stewart Island. Apart from populations in forests on Banks Peninsula, moreporks are uncommon in eastern South Island locations.

The birds also inhabit some suburban areas where there is cover in which to roost during the day. Moreporks roost during daylight hours in

Soon after dusk, a morepork captures a silvereye to share as the first meal of the night.

shaded locations, but when discovered in more visible roosts, small birds incessantly mob them, so that they are forced to find more secluded perches. This noisy mobbing often alerts birdwatchers to the location of a morepork.

As moreporks hunt at night, the birds often capture moths that have been attracted to streetlights in urban areas, in addition to their usual prey.

With their acute eyesight and hearing, as well as their completely silent flight, moreporks are extremely efficient night hunters. Their flight feathers are edged with a downy fringe, with the general plumage being soft. This completely muffles the sound of their flight when they approach their prey.

On one occasion, on a calm night, I was standing in a forest near a morepork's nest. I felt a puff of wind on my face, yet heard no sound, as the bird flew to its nest.

Top: Morepork with a captured mouse. As with the silvereye (previous page) and the decapitated sparrow (above) these form part of the first food to be offered to chicks at night.

Right: Insects, particularly weta, form the greater part of a morepork's diet and are usually brought to the nest in later night feeding.

No added nesting material is used in nest sites. Here a morepork has used a hollow beneath a clump of perching astelia in which to raise two chicks.

Most photographs of moreporks taken in daylight or in bright light show the golden yellow iris half-covering the eye, and this gives the birds a squinting appearance. However, as shown in some of the accompanying photographs, at night the iris is only partly visible.

Another interesting fact, revealed in the photograph on page 85, is that when a parent transfers food to a chick, the adult's eyes are often completely closed. This protects the large eyes from possible trauma.

Owls possess uncannily acute hearing, due in part to the fact that the external openings lie asymmetrically on the sides of the skull, and also to the feathery facial disc, which channels sound to the ears. In experiments, it has been shown that an owl can accurately locate the position of the most minimal sound made by a moving insect, even when the eyes have been masked.

The diet varies with location. Generally it consists of insects, varying in size from small moths to large beetles and stick insects. Moreporks are particularly fond of weta, a very common prey in native forests, and they also catch mice, geckos and small birds. Their first meal of the night often consists of a small bird which has not gone to roost at dusk.

Most of the food I have recorded taken after dark in mainland locations has been insects (particularly weta, huhu beetles and moths), and the occasional mouse. I have been unable to occupy observation hides at dawn when small birds are probably caught.

Like other birds that feed on mice, insects and smaller birds, moreporks frequently eject pellets of undigested material, which consists mostly of bones, fur and chitin (such as insects' wings). These pellets can be microscopically examined to determine accurately the prey on which the birds are feeding, although the frequency of feeding may not be known.

In milder regions of the mainland, particularly in northern districts, moreporks begin nesting in early October. The usual sites are dry hollows in trees, under bunches of perching astelia, on branches of large trees, or on beds of needles in the forks of very old pine trees. Nests have also been found on the ground in plantation forests, hidden beneath fern fronds. No additional nesting material is used in the nest site.

The female incubates the usual clutch of two eggs, with incubation beginning after the laying of the first egg. Of all the nests I have seen, the clutch has been of two eggs, but three-egg clutches have often been recorded.

I noticed that some nest sites were used again the following season. Although I have not used banding to identify moreporks, I believe that the same pair of birds probably reused a nesting site. In one case, a cavity in a puriri tree was used for two consecutive years (although when I checked the third year, I found a possum in residence and only fragments of broken eggshell in the nest).

There is considerable variation in the feeding and nesting behaviour of moreporks in captivity. In one zoo, probably due to the regular and adequate food supply, a pair nested in midwinter. Also, there is variation in the feeding behaviour of moreporks on small islands where their population may have reached capacity.

On small offshore islands, the diet is restricted to available food. On the Tiritiri Matangi Island reserve, moreporks take insects, and in the past also used to catch small kiore (Pacific rats). However, when the rats were eradicated from the

island, moreporks switched their large prey items to birds, some of which are caught before dark.

In addition to their common nocturnal call (which resembles 'morepork' or, to me, a sound like 'quor-co'), the birds also make many other calls, especially during the breeding season of late spring. Two such calls are a subdued repeated 'quor-quor-quor' and a vibrating, musical repeated 'cree-cree'.

It may be of interest to note here that one of the calls made by the spotted dove, when heard in the distance, might be mistaken for that of the morepork. However, the dove's calls would be heard only during the day.

When I first arrived in New Zealand in 1947, I found that, although moreporks' habits were generally documented, there was little in-depth information on their behaviour when nesting, apart from captive-bred birds. However, in 1948, I was given my first opportunity to study the morepork when notified by a local farmer who had heard frequent calls and activity in a nearby puriri tree. I climbed the tree and found a nest in a hollow beneath a clump of perching astelia, with a bird incubating two, almost round, white eggs.

Left: Three-week-old morepork chicks temporarily emerge from the nest to await food.

Above: When feeding older chicks, the adult may close its eyes to prevent damaging them.

Following pages: A stick insect is brought to the nest.

After the chicks had hatched, I built a hide about 3 metres from the nest. The sitting female was surprisingly confiding and did not appear alarmed at my building activities.

Since I was busy with my veterinary practice at that time I was restricted in how often I was able to use the hide, and did little photography, mainly making notes. Fortunately, the following year the birds, probably the same pair, used the same nest site and I was able to determine the incubation period of 30 days for the first chick to hatch. As incubation had started after the laying of the first egg, the second chick to hatch was considerably smaller than its sibling.

Left: A morepork flies to the nest with a moth to feed the waiting chicks.

Above: It can be seen clearly that the morepork's eyelid is completely closed, in anticipation of feeding the chick.

I spent the first session in the hide on a moonlit night, just watching the nesting activities. While it was still fairly light, I heard chattering and alarm cries of a blackbird and chattering of other birds and watched the male morepork land on a dead branch several metres to the left of my hide. He seemed to summon his mate, calling with a soft rippling, repeated 'cwree' call. The brooding female immediately became wide-eyed and after a short pause flew to the branch to join him.

After the repeated exchange of mewing sounds the male picked up the small bird he had caught in his talons. The female immediately snatched the prey from him and flew off with it in her beak. After eight minutes, without a sound, she landed at the nest, carrying the bird by its leg, having apparently eaten most of it herself. Then, gripping the prey with one foot, she proceeded to rip tiny portions of the flesh, which she very gently fed to the chicks. She swallowed the remaining indigestible portion herself and settled to brood the tiny chicks.

During the following hours, when the female remained on the nest, the male bird made frequent visits, bringing mainly small moths, which the female fed to the chicks. He usually announced his visits with a rippling call and made only a very brief visit to pass on the food.

After dark it was not possible for me to discern what activity occurred at the nest, so on subsequent visits to the hide I fitted a small torch bulb covered with red cellophane to the front of the hide. This gave just enough illumination to detect the main movements of the birds, but was insufficient to see any detail, or what prey was caught. It was only later, by examining the detail of my photographs taken with flash, that I was able to identify the prey accurately.

On each following occasion, I would occupy the hide at dusk, as the chatter of various small birds finding their night roosts was beginning to quieten, and set up my flash units and pre-focus the camera on the front of the nest. The female appeared to take no notice of my activity, only 3 metres from her nest site. In those early days I was using an old camera, which was loaded with quarter-plate glass negatives, and the flash unit was a Dawe, one of the first electronic units publicly available. It had the advantage of giving a very-high-speed, brief flash, which did not appear to be noticed by the birds.

Since it was so difficult to identify, let alone photograph, the food items that were being brought to the nest, I fixed a branch about a metre to the left of the nest, in the line of flight used by the male when bringing food. The perch proved its worth, as the male paused momentarily on the perch before taking the prey to the female, allowing me to photograph the food items.

In the following years I photographed activities at several nests, mainly located in tree cavities. In

most cases the first meal of the evening consisted of a bird, mouse or, on one occasion, a gecko. After dark, I noted that insects were the main items fed to the chicks, and as the chicks matured, very common prey fed to them were weta, huhu beetles or large moths. When chicks were a few weeks old and had been left alone all day, they sometimes ventured outside the nest hole to hungrily await their first meal of the night.

I witnessed the fledging of chicks on two occasions. The fledging period varied with different nests, probably depending on the food supply, but in most cases chicks fledge when they are approximately five weeks old. When the birds are about three weeks old they often clamber around the nest, exercising their wings.

The parents seem to sense when the chicks are ready to leave the nest. On each occasion after the

A weta is brought to feed to the chicks.

Morepork chicks, two and a half weeks old, emerge from the nest to await their first meal of the night.

chicks had been fed a few times into the night, one of the parents perched a few metres away from the nest hole and, carrying an item of food, called with a soft repeated 'cree-cree'. After much wing flapping, the older chick launched into its first flight and flew directly to perch near the parent. Not to be outdone, the younger, less well-developed chick took off, but ended up on the ground. Fearing it would be taken by predators, I left the hide, caught the chick and returned it to the safety of its nest. The next night it fledged successfully. A similar performance occurred at the second nest.

I believe that before mammalian predators were common in New Zealand, the less developed chick would have been fed on the ground by its parents until it was able to fly. This is similar behaviour to that of kaka chicks, which fledge before they can fly.

After fledging, the young moreporks remain with their parents for some weeks. On several occasions during daylight hours, I have seen both parents resting on a branch in a shady place, with two chicks, still with down protruding from their head feathers, perched between them. Late in the day, one could be led to their perch when hearing the sounds of their steamy, squeaky calls.

Much research is yet to be done on the nesting behaviour of moreporks. Fortunately, with the availability of sophisticated digital cameras, photographic records may be obtained without the need to spend many night hours in hides.

LITTLE OWL

Athene noctua

Widespread in pastoral South I.; not seen in North I.; locally common • Length: 23 cm • Status: Introduced

Above: Little owl parent takes a grub to feed chicks in the nest hole.

Below: A pair of little owls perched on a tree stump. These owls are often seen during daylight.

First introduced from Europe in 1906, the little owl, also known as the German owl, is widespread in eastern regions of the South Island. Apart from captive birds, it is not found in the North Island. The birds were introduced to help control small birds that were damaging fruit crops. It was subsequently proved, however, that little owls feed more frequently on insects.

The little owl does not exclusively inhabit native forests. It is a bird of the open country and farmland and may also be seen in small pine plantations and city parks. This species is included

Little owl chick at the entrance to the nest hole. A nest is often placed in the hollow of an old tree on the ground.

with forest birds as it sometimes nests in the hollows of trees on forest fringes, or in small stands of native trees. It is not thought to compete with the morepork for food, because it feeds mainly in open country habitats.

The little owl is slightly smaller and squatter than the morepork. It has a low, bouncing flight, which is often seen during daylight hours. It also often hunts in daylight, and I have seen birds perched in full sunlight on fence posts and power poles. Their call is a high-pitched 'tiew'.

Little owls feed mainly on insects and their larvae and are reported to take earthworms as they do in Europe, but this has not been observed in New Zealand. They also occasionally take lizards, mice and small birds. Although the birds may feed during the day, little owls more frequently hunt from dusk to dawn.

The birds usually nest low down in holes in trees, particularly willows, but also in holes on the ground, or among hay bales in farm buildings. No additional nesting material is used and the female incubates the clutch of two to four eggs for four weeks. Both parents feed the chicks, which fledge when they are about four and a half weeks old.

Order Coraciiformes

Kingfishers

Many species of kingfishers are distributed worldwide. However, New Zealand has only two forest kingfishers: the native New Zealand kingfisher and the uncommon, introduced Australian kookaburra.

The New Zealand kingfisher, *vagans*, is a subspecies of the Australian species, *Halcyon sancta*, which also inhabits New Guinea and many South Pacific islands.

The Australian kookaburra, introduced to Kawau Island by Sir George Grey in the 1860s, is uncommon and only inhabits the lower North Auckland region.

Although uncommon in large forests, the New Zealand kingfisher is included as a forest bird because it often chooses to feed and nest in forest habitats.

NEW ZEALAND KINGFISHER

Halcyon sancta vagans

Common; widespread • Protected
• Length: 24 cm • Maori name: kotare
• Status: Native

Kingfishers are common throughout most of New Zealand, particularly in sheltered marine habitats, open country and wetlands. Some birds inhabit forests where they feed and nest. Kingfishers are wary birds, and unless one is using a hide they are difficult to approach closely.

In forest habitats kingfishers feed on a variety of insects and grubs, as well as catching lizards and taking freshwater crayfish from forest streams. They also occasionally catch small birds.

Their usual contact call is a 'kek-kek', made five times, and during courtship a more musical, subdued 'kree-kree'. When boring their nest holes the birds utter short 'krek' calls as they fly to attack the tunnel entrance.

Although most New Zealand kingfishers inhabit coastal, wetland and agricultural locations, some birds feed and nest in the forest.

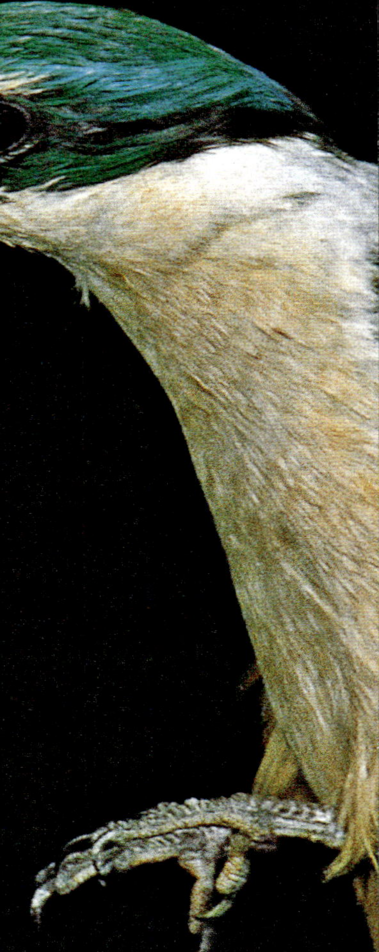

Nesting commences in September or October, and the birds start boring a nesting tunnel in a rotting or dead standing tree, or in a clay bank of a stream. In one forest a large tree, which had been blown over in a storm, had a mound of earth still adhering to its exposed roots. This area was riddled with the beginnings of nest borings, with many having been abandoned due to lack of depth of the earth. However, one successful tunnel was about 15 centimetres in length and ended in a nest chamber containing a clutch of six white eggs.

The female performs most of the incubating, which takes 21 days, although I have noticed males incubating for short periods when the female is off the nest feeding.

When chicks are first hatched, the parents take food items into the nest, but when they are about

Previous pages: Kingfisher flying to its nest with a cicada.

Right: As chicks age, they come to the nest entrance to be fed.

two weeks old chicks come to the entrance to receive food. All food portions taken by adults and larger chicks are swallowed whole, even large prey such as lizards or mice. However, large dragonflies and other insects are bashed on a branch to remove wings, and small birds or mice are beaten repeatedly to make them supple.

Like birds of prey, kingfishers will, at intervals, eject pellets of indigestible bones or chitin from insects. These pellets can later be examined microscopically to identify the food taken.

As chicks mature, they go to the nest entrance to defecate, and the area below the entrance soon becomes whitened. In addition, the wheezy, buzzing sound made by the older chicks often leads to the discovery of a kingfisher nest.

Observations made at several nests show that the first chicks to hatch leave the nest when 26 days old. They usually fly just a few metres to a branch where the male feeds them repeatedly until they gain strength. These first two or three chicks to fledge continue to be fed by the male and remain in the area with him for several days. The female continues to feed those chicks in the nest until they fledge.

Left: The kingfisher uses its tail for support as it feeds chicks at the nest hole.

Top: A newly fledged kingfisher stretching its wing.

Above: Kingfisher with a silvereye. Large prey is bashed repeatedly on a branch so that it can be swallowed easily.

Passerine birds

Almost half the birds of the world are classed in this order, which contains numerous suborders. Although birds in this classification are often referred to as passerine ('perching'), many birds in other orders are also able to perch.

All birds in the Passeriformes Order have four toes, with one permanently pointing backwards. In no cases are the toes webbed.

Chicks are altricial, meaning that they hatch helpless, naked and with their eyes closed. Some birds in other orders also share these features.

In New Zealand many forest-dwelling birds are included in this order. Seventeen species inhabit the forests of the North, South and Stewart Islands as well as some offshore islands. Those species that occupy the Chatham Islands and outlying islands are not included in this section.

RIFLEMAN
Acanthisitta chloris

Locally common • Length: 8 cm
• Maori name: titipounamu
• Status: Endemic

Two subspecies of the rifleman occupy New Zealand forests: *Acanthisitta chloris granti*, in the North Island, and *A. c. chloris*, in the South Island. They are the smallest birds that exist in New Zealand, favouring subalpine forests of both islands.

Riflemen are more common in the South Island, particularly in mixed mature forests and in the beech forests of north-west Nelson, Westland and Fiordland. They also inhabit some South Island forested offshore islands.

In the North Island, most riflemen inhabit forests south of the Waikato region. Other populations are found in the northland Warawara kauri forest and on Little Barrier and Great Barrier Islands; sightings of riflemen in the Coromandel have also been reported.

Riflemen are very territorial, even outside the nesting season, with pairs remaining in their territory throughout the year. They keep in contact with a high-pitched, repeated 'tsit-tsit'.

The birds feed on insects and their larvae and spiders, which they find among the bark and foliage of trees. They are usually seen feeding actively on prey in the bark and among moss and lichen. As they feed, riflemen often work in a

Left and below: Both rifleman parents are constantly busy as they search for spiders and insects for their chicks.

spiral motion, starting at the base of a tree and working upwards, with their wings constantly fluttering as they delve into crannies and flaking tree bark. Near the treetops, the birds drop down again and repeat the manoeuvre on another tree.

The tail and wing pattern of a South Island rifleman.

Riflemen have also been observed feeding on small ripe fruit.

During the nesting season, which extends from late September to January, the male seeks likely nesting sites, often choosing tree holes and sometimes crevices in banks. The nest cavity is lined with a few fragments of dry grasses or fern fronds and completed with the addition of a few feathers. The nest-hole crevice is surprisingly small. I measured the entrance of one hole in the trunk of an old beech tree in the Kaimanawa Mountains, finding it was less than 2 centimetres in diameter.

The female finally chooses one of the nests and lays two to four eggs, which are incubated in turn by both sexes for about 20 days. After the chicks hatch they are fed small insects at frequent intervals by both parents, as well as by helpers. These are thought to be chicks from an earlier nesting. Chicks fledge at about 24 days old.

WHITEHEAD
Mohoua albicilla

Locally common; North I. only • Protected • Length: 15cm • Maori name: popokotea, tataeko • Status: Endemic

The whitehead inhabits forest and scrub in the North Island, mainly south of the Waikato region. Prior to recent translocations, it was absent from the north apart from Little Barrier Island. Populations of whitehead have recently been introduced successfully to Tiritiri Matangi Island and the predator-managed area of the Waitakere Ranges, known as Ark in the Park. At the time of writing, further translocations are planned.

Whiteheads are insect feeders and are often seen in groups noisily feeding in the forest canopy. The birds often use their bills to flake off bark to expose insects. They also eat small fruit and seeds

Above: A whitehead and its nest in a mingimingi shrub. Most nests are built in shrubs.

Below: Whiteheads only inhabit the North Island.

This whitehead stood on the edge of the nest watching the chicks for several minutes.

from native trees. They make a 'swit' call, and during the nesting season males sing with a soft canary-like trill. During this nesting period, which extends from October to January, whiteheads are more likely to be seen in lower regions of the forest.

In shrubs or forks of trees, the birds build substantial nests composed of grasses, moss and lichen lined with tree-fern scales and a few feathers. The usual clutch of three pink-tinged eggs is incubated for 18 to 20 days. The female incubates and sometimes a 'helper' assists. This also occurs with the feeding of chicks, which fledge when they are about 20 days old. Helpers are probably older chicks from a previous brood.

I was once watching and photographing, from my hide, a whitehead at its nest in a mingimingi bush. The female was brooding small chicks. Suddenly, a violent thunderstorm broke with very heavy rain. The bird sat low on the nest with its wings slightly spread, so that the rain was diverted over the side of the nest.

The whitehead is one of the species used by the long-tailed cuckoo to incubate its egg and foster its chick.

YELLOWHEAD

Mohoua ochrocephala

Threatened; South I. only • Protected • Length: 15 cm • Maori name: mohua • Status: Endemic

Yellowhead numbers have declined in recent years. A few decades ago they were common in the beech forests of Fiordland, where I have photographed them in the Eglinton Valley. Due to predation by stoats, yellowheads are now extremely scarce in this area. The Department of Conservation is undertaking active predator control in Fiordland and hopes to maintain and enhance yellowhead populations in other South Island areas where they are more common.

Yellowheads have similar feeding habits to whiteheads, taking a variety of insects, their larvae and spiders. As they frequently find their prey on and within the flaked bark of trees, they use their tails as support, with the consequence that the

A yellowhead at the entrance of its nest in a cavity of a beech tree.

The endangered yellowhead inhabits South Island forests.

feathers become frayed.

Yellowheads nest from September to January. Their nests are of very similar construction to that of the closely related whitehead, but they are built in holes or shallow cavities on the trunk of a mature tree. For this reason, the incubating female is vulnerable to predation by stoats.

The clutch of two to four eggs is incubated for 20 days, and this task is sometimes shared by two females, possibly one being an earlier offspring. Males assist with feeding the chicks but do not share incubation. Chicks fledge when they are 21 days old.

BROWN CREEPER
Mohoua novaeseelandiae

Common; South I. only • Protected
• Length: 13 cm • Maori name: pipipi
• Status: Endemic

Brown creepers are common and widespread in South Island habitats of forest, manuka scrub and plantation pine forests. The birds are also seen on Stewart Island and some of its offshore islands. Brown creepers are also located up to the treeline in some alpine territories.

The birds are very active as they feed, taking varieties of insects, grubs and spiders, and are often seen hanging upside down taking prey from the underside of leaves. In winter months the birds flock to feed. Their contact call is a rapid 'chi-chi-chi-tee-tee'.

Brown creepers nest from September to January, and may rear three broods in a season. The second brood is selected by long-tailed cuckoos to

incubate their egg, with the brown creepers then serving as foster parents to the cuckoos' large chick.

Their nests are compact structures composed of fine dried grass, moss and lichen and bound with cobweb. Nests are usually well hidden in dense shrub or vine-covered matagouri. The clutch of two to four eggs is incubated for 17 days by the female, and chicks fledge when they are three weeks old.

Left: Brown creepers inhabit forest and scrub only in the South Island.

Above: Brown creepers are related to whiteheads and yellowheads.

GREY WARBLER

Gerygone igata

Common; widespread • Protected
• Length: 10 cm • Maori name: riroriro
• Status: Endemic

The grey warbler is one of our smallest birds, with a body size similar to a rifleman but possessing a longer tail. They were originally classified as warblers, but research by Brian Gill has shown them to be linked to songbirds.

Grey warblers are common and widespread, inhabiting native forest, scrub and some plantation forests where they feed on insects, their larvae and spiders. They are able to hover in flight and this enables them to pluck insects from the tips of stems and leaves, which are usually inaccessible to other insectivorous birds.

The birds have a sweet and melancholy song: a high-pitched trilling, tremulous warble, which often halts abruptly in mid-song.

They begin nesting in August, with the female building a pear-shaped, domed nest that has an entrance hole, 3 centimetres wide, at one side. The nest is attached to a branch in a way that allows it to swing freely, although often one side is attached to another branch that stabilises it.

Most nests consist of dried grasses, lichens, moss and shreds of bark and are strengthened with cobweb. The interior is thickly lined with feathers. One nest I observed being built consisted

Below: The common grey warbler is one of New Zealand's smallest birds.

Right: A grey warbler at its domed nest.

Above: This nest was largely composed of sheep's wool collected from a nearby wire fence.

Right and bottom right: Grey warblers are the only New Zealand birds to build a domed nest.

mainly of sheep's wool, which was plucked from a nearby barbed-wire fence.

It has been stated in some guidebooks that it takes 27 days for a nest to be completed, but my house once overlooked a row of Japanese cedar trees, which were favoured as nesting sites for blackbirds, thrushes, finches and grey warblers. Over the years, I was able to observe several grey warbler nests being built. Most of these were built in just eight or nine days.

Grey warblers lay a clutch of three or four eggs, each egg being laid at two-day intervals. The eggs are unusually large compared with the size of the bird. The female incubates them for 20 days, and the chicks fledge when they are nearly three weeks old, although they remain with, and are fed by, the parents for several days.

Up to three broods are reared in a season, but the second nesting is usually commandeered by the shining cuckoo, which lays one egg in each of several grey warbler nests. There is still research to be done on the number of nests used and the manner in which the cuckoo deposits its egg in the domed nest. Some exotic cuckoos lay their egg on the ground and carry it in their beak to deposit it in the nest. Others lay directly into the nest. As far as the grey warblers' domed nest is concerned, the egg may be ejected into the nest with the cuckoo gripping the sides of the entrance hole.

The incubation period of the cuckoo egg is much shorter than that of the grey warbler, so when the cuckoo chick is about three days old, it is able to eject the warbler eggs from the nest. This allows the cuckoo chick to dominate the nest and receive full attention from the grey warbler pair.

After fledging, the shining cuckoo chick, which is considerably larger than its foster parents, makes considerable demands on the grey warblers, calling incessantly for food.

FANTAIL

Rhipidura fuliginosa

Common; widespread • Protected • Length: 16 cm • Maori name: piwakawaka, tiwakawaka • Status: Native

The fantail inhabits islands of the Pacific region, including Australia, with two subspecies occurring in New Zealand. The North Island subspecies, *Rhipidura fuliginosa placabilis*, is common throughout the North Island, inhabiting forest, scrub, residential gardens, parks and open country where trees are present. The subspecies *R. f. fuliginosa* is common in the South and Stewart Islands, inhabiting forests, scrub and farming areas, but scarce in the drier areas of Marlborough and Otago. The South Island population is dimorphic in colour, with the plumage of approximately 20 per cent of the fantails being sooty-black.

Fantails are insectivorous, feeding on a wide range of insects, including flies, mosquitoes,

Below: Black fantails are common in the South Island.

beetles and moths. The bristles around their bills assist the birds to catch insects in flight, and, using their fanned tails, the birds sweep across foliage to dislodge insects. They are adept at capturing varieties of insects on the wing. During winter months, fantails often flock together, feeding on grass pastures in farmland where they catch insects that have been disturbed by the hooves of cattle.

Fantails often rear four or five broods in a season, with the first nests being built in August. In the North Island the female alone builds nests, but in South Island locations males often assist in nest building. The compact nest is composed of dry grasses, moss, lichen and fern scales that are bound together with cobweb, and a tail of nest material is left trailing from the base. The nest takes about seven or eight days to be completed;

however, I watched one female complete a nest in four days, and then she laid the first egg of a clutch of three the following morning.

Incubation, which is shared by the sexes, takes 14 days. On one occasion, I observed an incubating bird that would not vacate the nest, and then its mate actually sat on top of the sitting bird for two minutes before the sitting bird vacated the nest. Chicks fledge when they are 14

Far left: A typical fantail nest has a long tail.

Middle top: A female fantail building her nest. The nest was completed in four days.

Middle bottom: Fantail brooding older chicks.

Above: A fantail feeding chicks.

or 15 days old. But nests with four chicks are so cramped that chicks fledge earlier and perch together on a nearby branch to be fed frequently by the parents.

If incubation begins on a subsequent brood, one parent feeds the earlier chicks, still perched together on a nearby branch.

Previous pages: Parents feed the fledged chicks.

Above: When more than three chicks occupy a nest they usually fledge early to a nearby branch and are fed repeatedly, so they will quickly gain strength to fly well.

Left: Three older chicks bulge in the nest.

NEW ZEALAND TOMTIT

Petroica macrocephala

Common; widespread • Protected
• Length: 13 cm • Maori names: miromiro
(North I.), ngirungiru (South I.)
• Status: Endemic

Two subspecies of the endemic tomtit inhabit mainland New Zealand, Stewart Island and offshore islands. The North Island subspecies, *Petroica macrocephala toitoi*, is found throughout forest areas and the larger offshore islands, but it is uncommon in the Manawatu and Wairarapa.

The South Island subspecies, *P. m. macrocephala*, is common in most forest regions, including plantation forests and on Stewart Island, as well as forest regions on Banks Peninsula. However, the birds are uncommon in drier districts of Marlborough and eastern regions of the South Island.

Above: A South Island male tomtit, showing its pied plumage.

Below: A drab-coloured female tomtit sits at the nest.

North Island tomtits have a white breast, whereas the male South Island tomtits, especially in the nesting season, show a smudge of yellow on the upper breast.

Tomtits are insectivorous, catching a wide variety of insects from the bark and foliage of trees and, occasionally, among the litter on the forest floor. As they usually feed in the upper canopy of the forest they do not seriously compete with robins, which tend to feed in the lower canopy and on the ground.

Tomtits sing with a warbling 'ti-oly–ti-oly' song, and use a short high-pitched 'zee-zee' contact call. In the bush, usually only the male tomtit makes itself apparent to human intruders.

Nesting starts in September and second broods are raised in December and January. Nests are constructed of mosses, lichen and pieces of bark bound with cobweb. The nests are usually difficult to locate as they merge with the tree trunk, or are built in crevices or in the hollows of broken branches. I have also found nests in depressions of mossy banks and, in northern forests, often on the side of a tree fern trunk.

Top: A female North Island tomtit sits at the nest.

Above: Tomtit chicks close to fledging.

The female incubates the clutch of three or four eggs for 16 days, and chicks fledge when they are 16 days old. The female builds a second nest, leaving the male to continue rearing the chicks in the first nest.

NEW ZEALAND ROBIN
Petroica australis

Common; widespread • Protected
• Length: 18 cm • Maori name: toutouwai
• Status: Endemic

The North Island robin, *Petroica australis longipes*, is common on Little Barrier and Kapiti Islands, but this subspecies has a patchy distribution on the mainland. The birds are reasonably common in native and some plantation forests in the central North Island and the Ureweras. Introductions have been made to predator-controlled 'mainland island' refuges including the Waitakere Ranges' Ark in the Park, where the birds have also nested successfully.

The South Island robin, *P. a. australis*, is common in native and exotic pine forests of Nelson and Marlborough, south of the Arthur's Pass, and Okarito forests. They also inhabit the beech forests of eastern Fiordland.

Robins are very territorial and sing from high perches with an outpouring of warbles that rise and fall in volume. They sometimes sing without a break for long periods. When recording their song in the Kowhai Bush near Kaikoura, a colleague, Ken Bigwood, recorded one robin which sang without pause for an hour and five minutes.

A North Island robin. These birds are confiding and often feed among leaf litter. They may perch close to a walkway, being attracted to overturned stones and leaves.

Robins feed on a variety of invertebrates, even taking weta and stick insects. They can be attracted to take insects on the ground by disturbing leaf litter. The birds also use a foot in a trembling motion on the ground to attract earthworms to the surface.

Robins nest from September to January, building substantial nests of grasses, rootlets, moss and lichen, sometimes reinforced with cobweb. The nests are usually built in the fork of a tree or bush, and sometimes in a shallow crevice of a large tree.

The usual clutch consists of two to four eggs, which are incubated by the female for 18 days. The male frequently calls her from the nest to feed her and visits the nest to feed the chicks after they hatch. Early in the season, when chicks are about two weeks old, the birds nest again. The female then leaves the male to care for these earlier chicks while she makes another nest. Chicks fledge when they are 21 days old.

As robins frequently feed on the ground, they are very susceptible to being caught by mammalian predators.

Far left: Robins often feed on insects and earthworms on the forest floor, making them vulnerable to predation.

Top left: A robin's nest in the shelter of a broken tree limb.

Bottom left: After feeding chicks, the faecal sac is removed to maintain a clean nest.

Above: A robin feeding chicks. The male continues to feed the chicks when the female makes another nest.

Right: A pair of North Island robins at their nest.

SILVEREYE

Zosterops lateralis lateralis

Abundant; widespread • Protected
• Length: 12 cm • Maori name: tauhou
• Status: Native

Silvereyes, also known as white-eyes or waxeyes, first arrived in New Zealand in 1856, from Australia. It is thought that they were probably assisted in their migration by perching on the rigging of the many sailing ships crossing the Tasman at that time.

The birds inhabit mixed and regenerating forests, as well as scrub, mangroves, orchards and suburban gardens. They often do damage to orchard fruits and vineyards, but are also useful in that they eat aphids and other garden pests.

Their diet consists of caterpillars, spiders and even quite large insects. I photographed one feeding a katydid to its chicks. They also take nectar from several flowering species, and in parts of the South Island birds migrate in very large flocks to feed where the South Island rata is in bloom. In winter months silvereyes congregate in large flocks to feed in forests and gardens. They

Top left: Silvereye in flight.

Bottom left: A silvereye (or white-eye). The birds are common in forest or scrub, but also visit suburban gardens.

Above and right: Silvereyes build nests suspended within shrubs and branches. Composed of grasses, moss and lichen, the nests are tightly woven with spider's web.

Below: Silvereye chicks being fed with a katydid.

will readily visit garden bird tables to feed on sugar water.

Apart from damaging ripe orchard fruit, silvereyes also eat many smaller whole fruits, and I have photographic records of them feeding whole inkweed fruits to their chicks. In this way they are responsible for spreading weed seeds.

Silvereyes rear several broods in a season, from September to February. Their nests are usually flimsy, hammock-like structures composed of grasses, lichen, moss and small dry leaves. They are typically built in shrubs, on the ends of pine-tree branches or in bamboo. Both sexes share incubation of the clutch of three or four eggs for 11 days, and chicks fledge when they are 11 or 12 days old. They remain as a family group until another nest is built.

STITCHBIRD

Notiomystis cincta

Highly endangered; offshore islands and mainland refuges • Length: 18 cm • Maori name: hihi • Status: Endemic

The stitchbird is the smallest and rarest of the true honeyeaters. It was formerly listed with tui and bellbird in the family Meliphagidae, but as a result of recent DNA tests is now listed in a separate family, the Notiomystidae.

Until the late nineteenth century the stitchbird inhabited forests of the North Island, but the mainland population became extinct due to predation by introduced mammalian predators and avian diseases. It survived only on Little Barrier Island. Following the elimination of feral cats and rats from the Little Barrier sanctuary, the population of stitchbirds increased. This has allowed transfers of individuals to other predator-free islands, and, at the time of writing, stitchbirds have also been transferred to the predator-controlled Ark in the Park, in the Waitakere Ranges. Here, some pairs have bred successfully within months of their introduction to the flora-rich environment.

Stitchbirds were so named as a result of their very high-pitched single call. They also produce a call sounding like 'see-zip'. They are smaller than tui and bellbirds, and are often prevented by these birds from accessing many of the nectar-bearing flowers and fruits. When becoming established in a new habitat they have to be supplied with artificial sugar water in special feeding tables covered with netting that excludes bellbirds. In addition to nectar and fruit, stitchbirds also feed on insects, their larvae and spiders, especially to provide necessary protein when feeding chicks. Chicks require protein from insect food to maintain growth. They would not survive on a diet lacking in protein. Adults also need the extra protein to produce eggs.

Male stitchbird (left), and female stitchbird (above) with a coprosma fruit.

Stitchbirds are the only honeyeaters known to nest in holes in trees. Their nests of sticks, tree-fern scales and small dry leaves are lined with feathers and usually built above the entrance hole. They produce several broods in the season, which extends from September to March.

The female incubates the clutch of two to four eggs for 15 days, and the chicks fledge when they are about four weeks old. There is often a high mortality of stitchbirds in winter months, resulting from a week or two of a scarcity or absence of food. The nectar-bearing plants or fruits on which they feed are often taken by the more aggressive bellbird, with the result that the stitchbirds may starve.

BELLBIRD

Anthornis melanura melanura

Common, except Northland; widespread • Protected • Length: 20 cm • Maori names: korimako, makomako • Status: Endemic

The endemic bellbird is widely distributed throughout most of New Zealand and its offshore islands. Although there are thriving populations on Northland's offshore islands, bellbirds are absent from the mainland north of Auckland, apart from winter visits by male birds.

Until the late nineteenth century bellbirds inhabited Northland, but avian diseases spread by introduced European birds probably decimated the population. The destruction was most likely aided by the presence of ship rats. But, as rat infestations were present in other regions where bellbirds survived, it would seem that localised disease was the main factor in their demise.

Bellbirds are particularly noted for their

melodious song, best heard when several birds join in a dawn chorus. Bellbirds are one of the few species whose song can be heard through most months of the year, although less frequently so during moulting.

The birds inhabit native forests and scrublands, as well as city parks and suburban gardens. Being honeyeaters, they feed on many exotic flowering garden plants. Female bellbirds take more insect food than males, as dominant males tend to chase females from nectar-bearing native trees. In autumn and winter months, bellbirds take small fruit as well as insects.

Bellbirds rear two broods a season, with the first in September. Their well-hidden nests are deep cups composed of small sticks and dried grasses and lined with a few feathers. The female incubates the clutch of three or four eggs for a period of 15 days.

Most nests on the mainland and on Kapiti Island are built in thick shrubs, but on Hen Island all the nests I found were built in crevices of trees. This nest-site selection has probably evolved over the centuries to protect the nests from destruction by petrels and shearwaters, which crash into the forests when visiting their nesting burrows at night.

Both parents feed the chicks, mainly on insects and occasional fruit. I have noticed variations in the fledging times of chicks, which usually takes 14 to 16 days, something that may depend on the food available.

Left: The female bellbird with a white stripe below the eye and duller plumage.

Bottom left: A male bellbird.

Above: Both parents feed the chicks, firstly on nectar, then insects and fruit.

TUI

Prosthemadera novaeseelandiae novaeseelandiae

Common; widespread • Protected • Length: 30 cm • Status: Endemic

Tui are the largest of New Zealand's honeyeaters. They inhabit forests, open country with trees, urban parks and gardens.

The birds are strong fliers, with their noisy flight being produced by a notch in the eighth primary feather of the wing. Tui can often be seen flying high above the canopy of the bush, perhaps catching moths or other flying insects on the wing.

These birds are responsible for pollinating many native flowers; flax plants are a favourite and they can often be seen with flax pollen colouring their heads. Tui consume the smaller

fruit of podocarp trees such as kahikatea and play an important role in dispersing the whole seeds of these trees. Exotic flowering shrubs and trees attract tui to suburban gardens, where they will also take sugar water from an artificial bowl.

Male tui are larger than females and are aggressive towards them when feeding on a favourite tree with nectar-bearing flowers. Particularly in the nesting season, the birds also feed on a variety of insects, both small and large.

In the breeding season tui are very territorial, but after nesting, small flocks will often gather and fly to some nectar-bearing trees.

Tui usually rear two broods a year, with the first nest being built in September or October. The female builds a bulky nest of sticks, lining it with softer grasses. On predator-free islands, nests are often built in forks of trees or in the crowns of tree ferns. These sites would be predated easily on the mainland, but here most nests are built in thick shrubs and leafy branches of large trees, particularly in the upper levels of kanuka.

The clutch of three or four eggs is incubated by the female for 14 to 16 days, and chicks fledge when they are about 21 days old. Both parents feed the chicks, and do so extremely rapidly, which can make it difficult to identify the food being given. However, by photographing with a high-speed flash it is possible to identify most food items. These are mainly podocarp fruits and insects, with nectar and tiny insects in the early stages, followed by large insects when the chicks are older. After fledging, the chicks are still occasionally fed by the parents.

I once photographed three-day-old chicks

Top left: A tui nest in the low fork of a tree on a predator-free island. The vulnerable nest would have been predated on the mainland.

Bottom left: Like bellbirds, tui feed on nectar and fruit. Insects are taken more particularly when nesting, to provide protein to chicks.

Above: Male tui are sometimes aggressive when feeding, even denying females access to nectar.

being fed tiny insects. The second chick was fed before the first had time to even close its gape or swallow the insect.

On one occasion, when the chicks were over two weeks old, I used a 16 mm movie camera set on slow motion (80 fps) to record a parent bringing a large stick insect as food. The insect was thrust into the wide-open gape of the first chick. It was unable to swallow it. The parent then fed it to the second chick with the same result, and when the third chick was unable to swallow the large insect, the parent left the nest, taking the unpalatable stick insect, which it probably devoured itself.

In suburban gardens young chicks are very vulnerable to predation by domestic cats.

Left: This tui nest on Hen Island off the Northland east coast appears to have been rebuilt several times.

Below: Chicks are fed mainly by the female, although the male makes occasional visits.

KOKAKO

Callaeas cinerea

Endangered; North I. only • Protected
• Length: 38 cm • Status: Endemic

The North Island kokako, *Callaeas cinerea wilsoni*, survives in a few localised mature forests in Northland, the Urewera region, North Taranaki and localised areas near Rotorua. A few pairs were surviving in Coromandel forests, but they have recently been eliminated, probably by mammalian predators. Areas where pests have been controlled, such as Mapara, Pureora and the Hunua Ranges, support better populations. Due to translocations, good populations of kokako inhabit Little Barrier Island and some predator-free offshore islands.

The South Island kokako, *C. c. cinerea*, is now considered to be extinct, although there have been occasional reported sightings.

Kokako are renowned for their hauntingly beautiful song, best heard at dawn. Some notes resemble those of a tui, but the kokako's song is usually a series of long, melodic organ-like notes,

A North Island kokako. The birds are often secretive, being more frequently seen at dawn, when they perch to sing in the open.

Top left: Kokako are weak fliers and rarely fly any distance within the forest.

Top right: A kokako singing at dawn.

Above: During courtship the male kokako offers his mate a token of fruit.

followed by mews, flute calls and repeated clucks.

Kokako tend to choose a favourite prominent tree in which to sing, usually at dawn. However, some years ago, in forest bordering the Hautaru East road in western Waikato, I heard birdsong during the early afternoon. Thinking it must be a particularly melodious tui song, I entered the bush, following the call, and located a kokako singing from a high branch in a rimu tree.

Kokako are weak fliers. With their short, rounded wings they usually bound from tree to tree with their powerful legs, using their wings for balance or making short glides from one branch to another. They are very rarely seen in open flight. For this reason it is important to provide forested corridors to connect isolated areas of forest.

I filmed an unusually long flight of a kokako, in a forest remnant, coincidentally named Mt Kokako, north of the Hamilton–Raglan road. A steep, tree-covered valley remained in this recently

Top: Parents share feeding of the chicks. Above: Feeding a chick with a supplejack fruit.

Previous pages: Kokako parents feeding chicks.

Above: After a few visits to feed the chicks, the female cleans the nest and then preens the chicks.

logged forest where a lone male kokako sang his haunting dawn melody. With my 16 mm movie camera, I recorded this frustrated bird in level flight for 90 metres.

Kokako feed mainly on fruit, succulent foliage and flowers, but also take insects, particularly when feeding their chicks. They suffer competition for food in forests where possums are also present.

When the habitat is predator-free and food is plentiful, kokako often raise two broods of chicks in a season, the first nest usually being built in late October. Nests are bulky structures built by the female. They consist of a base of sticks, overlaid with fern fronds, lichen and mosses and built in trees or tall shrubs that are often draped with vines. The female incubates the usual clutch of two, or sometimes three, eggs for 20 to 21 days. She broods the newly hatched chicks for the first few days, with the male visiting the nest to bring food.

As the chicks develop, displaying at first lilac-coloured wattles, the female appears to do most of the feeding, making an average of three visits to the nest with food, compared with one visit by the male. When the chicks mature and become feathered, the female brings food to them two or three times, then vigorously cleans the bottom of the nest and often preens the chicks.

When feeding the chicks, the adult's head movements are so rapid that it is difficult to identify most food items. However, using high-speed flash exposures to freeze the rapid movements, it is possible to later identify the food being fed to the chicks. One example was an item that appeared to the eye to be green vegetable matter, but later proved to be green scale insects.

I had previously watched a kokako with a branchlet of pate (*Schefflera digitata*) leaves. The kokako held this on a branch to steady it while picking the insects from the underside of the leaves. I was once able to retrieve and identify some of the insects, which had been inadvertently dropped on the edge of the nest.

When about four to four and a half weeks old the chicks leave the nest, but they stay with the parents for several weeks, occasionally being offered food by the parents while learning to find their own food.

SADDLEBACK

Philesturnus carunculatus

Rare; offshore island sanctuaries • Protected • Length: 25 cm • Maori name: tieke • Status: Endemic

Saddlebacks are related to other wattlebirds such as kokako and the extinct huia. The wattles refer to the coloured appendages that are attached near the birds' throats. These are large in males, smaller in females.

At the time of European settlement, saddlebacks were common in forested areas throughout the North, South and Stewart Islands. They also inhabited many forested offshore islands. However, as the birds often feed on the ground in search of food, they were particularly vulnerable to predation by the mammalian pests introduced by early settlers.

Until quite recently, good populations of the South Island saddleback, *Philesturnus carunculatus carunculatus*, survived on Big South Cape Island and on a few smaller islands off the south coast of Stewart Island. However, in the 1960s ship rats were inadvertently introduced to Big South Cape Island by muttonbirders, and large numbers of saddlebacks were preyed upon. A rescue operation by the Department of Conservation saved a comparatively small number of the birds. These were translocated to many other offshore islands, but with only limited success.

Today, the South Island saddleback is an endangered subspecies. In contrast, the North Island saddleback, *P. c. rufusater*, has made a very successful recovery.

In 1964, I was fortunate to join a Wildlife Department expedition to study the habits of the saddleback, as at that time little was known of its feeding habits. The only population of North Island saddlebacks survived on Hen Island, in the Hen and Chickens group off the east coast of Northland. The island was free of mammalian predators, apart from the kiore rat. It was found that the birds fed mainly on insects from foliage and the bark of trees, but also spent almost 30 per cent of their time feeding among the leaf litter on the forest floor. This habit made them particularly vulnerable to predation on mainland habitats.

A male North Island saddleback.

North Island saddlebacks have since been very successfully relocated from their last stronghold on Hen Island to many North Island predator-free islands. At the time of writing, some are being considered for release on some 'mainland island' refuges.

When feeding, saddlebacks hold large insects (such as weta, stick insects or case moth larvae) in one foot, parrot fashion, and with their strong bills pull off and eat the succulent parts. Saddlebacks also take nectar and ripe fruit, particularly the small fruit of shrubs and podocarp trees.

Following the team's study of the saddleback's feeding and nesting habits, several successful translocations of the birds to other predator-free islands were made. Today, good populations inhabit many large and small offshore islands.

At night, saddlebacks roost in the safety of crevices and holes of large trees. The birds rear several broods in a season, with the usual clutch comprising two to four eggs. The first nests are built in September by the female and consist of small sticks and dried grasses placed in the hollow or deep crevice of a tree. They also use artificial nest boxes provided for them.

Incubation by the female lasts for 18 days. During this time, the male calls her from the nest to be fed on insects and grubs. Depending on the stage of incubation of the eggs, she is usually off the nest for 10 to 15 minutes, and I have observed females drinking as well, and on two occasions taking a bath.

Chicks fledge when they are about three weeks old and accompany the parents until the birds re-nest, but at nests late in the season the birds will often feed as a family group.

Right: A female saddleback approaches the hole entrance to her nest.

Below: A saddleback holding a case moth with one foot while extracting the larva (grub).

Above: A male saddleback calls the female from the nest to feed her. Below left: He feeds her on a nearby branch.

Below right: After feeding, the female saddleback sometimes bathes before returning to the nest.

GLOSSARY

Altricial Hatched without feathers, with eyes closed, and relying totally on parents for warmth and food.
Brood To sit over chicks to keep them warm.
Chitin The indigestible material of crustacean shells and insect wings.
Cosmopolitan Inhabiting many countries.
Crepuscular Active at dawn and dusk.
Dimorphic Showing two distinct forms, especially of plumage, among birds of the same species.
Diurnal Active during the day.
Endemic Living and breeding in New Zealand, and confined solely to the New Zealand region (e.g. brown kiwi).
Feral A domesticated animal that has become wild.
Fledged Fully feathered and able to fly.
Flight feathers The long, well-developed feathers of the wing and tail; the primary and secondary feathers of the wing.
Hawk To hunt or attempt to capture, especially on the wing.
Honeydew A sweetish liquid excreted by sap-sucking insects.
Introduced Brought into New Zealand from elsewhere, whether self-introduced or by human agency (e.g. the little owl, first introduced from Europe in 1906).
Invertebrates Animals without a spinal column (e.g. earthworms, insects, spiders).
Juvenile Young bird in its first plumage.
Mustelid Member of the family Mustelidae (e.g. stoat, ferret, weasel).
Native Naturally occurring in New Zealand, and breeding here, but also found elsewhere in the world (e.g. shining cuckoo, which arrives each September from the Solomon Islands, islands of the Bismarck Archipelago, and some other Pacific Islands).
Precocial Able to display independent activity at birth, especially birds that are hatched covered with down and with open eyes.
Raptor A bird of prey.
Subspecies A geographical population of a species, bearing some slight differences from others of the same species.
Threatened (A species that is) declining or low in numbers and at risk or serious decline or extinction.

FURTHER READING

Atlas of Bird Distribution in New Zealand. Wellington: Ornithological Society of New Zealand, 2007.

Checklist of the Birds of New Zealand. Fourth edition, Wellington: Te Papa Press with the Ornithological Society of New Zealand, in press (April 2010).

Buller, Walter L., *Manual of the Birds of New Zealand.* Government Printer, 1882.

Heather, Barrie and Robertson, Hugh, *Field Guide to the Birds of New Zealand.* Auckland: Viking, 2000.

Moon, Geoff, *A Photographic Guide to Birds of New Zealand.* Auckland: New Holland, 2002.

Moon, Lynnette (photographs by Geoff Moon), *Know Your New Zealand Birds.* Auckland: New Holland, 2006.

INDEX

Acanthisitta chloris 100–02
chloris chloris 100
chloris granti 100
Anthornis melanura melanura 23, 126–7
Apteryx australis 11, 26–9
australis australis 26
australis lawryi 26
australis mantelli 26
haastii 32
owenii 30–2
Athene noctua 93–4

bellbird 23, 126–7
blackbird 25

Cacatua galerita 54
Callaeas cinerea cinerea 131–6
cinerea wilsoni 131–6
chaffinch 25
Chrysococcyx lucidus lucidus 73–5
cockatoo, sulphur-crested 54
cockatoos 54
creeper, brown 106–07
cuckoo, long-tailed 76–7
shining 73–5
cuckoos 73
Cyanoramphus auriceps auriceps 68–70
malherbi 70
novaezelandiae novaezelandiae 61–7

diurnal birds of prey 34
dove, barbary 43
Malaysian spotted 43
doves 43

Eudynamys taitensis 76–7
Falco cenchroides cenchroides 34
novaeseelandiae 19, 34–7

falcon, New Zealand 19, 34–7
falcons 34
fantail 18, 111–16
forest birds 22–5
forests, birds in 22–5
modification of 9–13
New Zealand 8–25
types of 18–21

Gallirallus australis 38–42
australis australis 38
australis greyi 38
australis hectori 38
australis scotti 38
Gerygone igata 108–11

Halcyon sancta vagans 95–9
Hemiphaga chathamensis 43
novaeseelandiae novaeseelandiae 23, 43–53
hihi 23, 124–5

introduced birds 25

kaka 18, 23
North Island 14, 55–9
South Island 60
kakapo 54
kakariki 61–7, 68–70
karearea 19, 34–7
kereru 23, 43–53
kestrel, Nankeen 34
kingfisher, New Zealand 95–9
kingfishers 95
kiwi, brown 11, 26–9
great spotted 32
25, 26
little spotted 30–2
kiwi-pukupuku 30–2
koekoea 76–7
kokako 18, 23, 131–6
kookaburra, Australian 95
korimako 23, 126–7
kotare 95–9
kukupa 23, 43–53
makomako 23, 126–7
miromiro 117–18

Mohoua albicilla 103–05
novaeseelandiae 106–07
ochrocephala 105–06
mohua 105–06
morepork 78–92

Nestor meridionalis meridionalis 60
meridionalis septentrionalis 55–59
ngirungiru 117–18
Ninox novaeseelandiae 78–92
Notiomystis cincta 23, 124–5

owl, Australian barn 78
little 93–4
morepork 78–92
owls 78

parakeet, orange-fronted 70
red-crowned 61–7
yellow-crowned 18, 68–70
parakeets 18, 54
parea 43
parrots 54
passerine birds 100
petrel, Cook's 22
grey-faced 22
Petroica australis 25, 119–21
australis australis 119
australis longipes 119
macrocephala 117–18
macrocephala macrocephala 117–18
macrocephala toitoi 117–18
Philesturnus carunculatus 13, 18, 23, 25, 137–9
carunculatus carunculatus 137
carunculatus rufusater 137
pigeon, Chatham Island 43
New Zealand 23, 43–53
pigeons 43
pipipi 106–07
pipiwharauroa 73–5
piwakawaka 18, 111–16
Platycercus eximius 70–72
popokotea 103–05
Prosthemadera novaeseelandiae novaeseelandiae 23, 128–30

rails 38
Rhipidura fuliginosa 18, 111–16
fuliginosa fuliginosa 111
fuliginosa placabilis 111
rifleman 100–02
riroriro 108–10
roa 32
robin, New Zealand 25, 119–21
rosella, eastern 70–72
rowi 11, 26–9
ruru 78–92

saddleback 13, 18, 23, 25, 137–9
silvereye 18, 23, 122–3
starling 25
stitchbird 23, 124–5
Streptopelia chinensis tigrina 43
roseogrisea 43
Strigops habroptilus 54

tataeko 103–05
tauhou 18, 23, 122–3
tieke 13, 18, 23, 25, 137–9
titipounamu 100–02
tiwakawaka 18, 111–16
tokoeka 11, 26–9
tomtit 25, 117–18
toutouwai 25, 119–21
tui 23, 128–30
Tyto alba delicatula 78

warbler, grey 18, 108–11
waxeye 18, 23, 122–3
weka 38–42
buff 38
North Island 38
Stewart Island 38
western 38
white-eye 18, 23, 122–3
whitehead 103–05
woodhen 38–42

yellowhead 105–06

Zosterops lateralis lateralis 18, 23, 122–3

First published in 2010 by New Holland Publishers (NZ) Ltd
Auckland • Sydney • London • Cape Town

www.newhollandpublishers.co.nz

218 Lake Road, Northcote, Auckland 0627, New Zealand
Unit 1, 66 Gibbes Street, Chatswood, NSW 2067, Australia
86–88 Edgware Road, London W2 2EA, United Kingdom
80 McKenzie Street, Cape Town 8001, South Africa

Publishing manager: Matt Turner
Editor: Brian O'Flaherty
Design: Dexter Fry

National Library of New Zealand Cataloguing-in-Publication Data

Moon, Geoff.
New Zealand forest birds and their world / Geoff Moon,
completed under the direction of Lynnette Moon.
Includes bibliographical references and index.
ISBN 978-1-86966-196-0
1. Forest birds—New Zealand—Pictorial works. 2. Forest birds—
New Zealand. I. Moon, Lynnette. II. Title.
598.0993—dc 22
10 9 8 7 6 5 4 3 2 1

Colour reproduction by Pica Digital Pte Ltd., Singapore
Printed in China by Toppan Leefung Printing Ltd, on paper sourced from sustainable forests.

Front cover: New Zealand pigeon or kereru
Acknowledgements page: The author at a falcon hide
Contents page: New Zealand falcon or karearea
Back cover (l–r): Five-day-old brown kiwi leaving its burrow for the first time; Kahikatea forest, Westland; morepork with weta prey

Also from New Holland Publishers

Know Your New Zealand Birds
Lynnette Moon, photographs Geoff Moon
ISBN 978 1 86966 089 5

A Field Guide to New Zealand Seabirds
(second edition)
Brian Parkinson
ISBN 978 1 86966 150 2

Where to Watch Birds in New Zealand
Kathy Ombler
ISBN 978 1 86966 154 0

Birds of New Zealand Checklist
Brian O'Flaherty
ISBN 978 1 86966 119 9

A Photographic Guide to Birds of New Zealand
Geoff Moon
ISBN 978 1 877246 58 6

New Zealand Wetland Birds and their World
Geoff Moon
ISBN 978 1 86966 197 7